W9-ARU-562

CREATIVE IDEAS
FOR HOUSEHOLD STORAGE

THE HOMEOWNER'S LIBRARY

CREATIVE IDEAS FOR HOUSEHOLD STORAGE

Graham Blackburn
and the Editors of Consumer Reports Books

Consumers Union
Mount Vernon, New York

Copyright © 1990 by Graham Blackburn
All rights reserved, including the right
of reproduction in whole or in part in any form.

Library of Congress Cataloging-in-Publication Data
Blackburn, Graham, 1940–
Creative ideas for household storage / Graham Blackburn and the
editors of Consumer Reports Books.
p.   cm. — (The Homeowner's library)
ISBN 0-89043-294-5
1. Cabinet-work. 2. Storage in the home. I. Consumer Reports
Books. II. Title. III. Series.
TT197.B583   1990
684.1'6—dc20   89–78067
                                                              CIP
ISBN: 0-89043-294-5

Design by GDS / Jeffrey L. Ward
Illustrations by Graham Blackburn
First Printing, May 1990
Manufactured in the United States of America

Consumer Reports Books

Christopher J. Kuppig	Director
Sarah Uman	Executive Editor
Roslyn Siegel	Acquisitions Editor
Peter Bejger	Editorial Consultant
Tom Blum	Assoc. Acquisitions Editor
Julie Henderson	Assoc. Acquisitions Editor
Neil R. Wells	Editorial Assistant
Meta Brophy	Editorial Production Manager
Benjamin Hamilton	Production Editor
Marlene Tungseth	Production Editor
Jane Searle	Production Coordinator
Michele Harris	Director of Marketing and Sales
Helene Kaplan	Sr. Marketing Analyst
Christopher Martin	Marketing Assistant
Matthew McDade	Marketing Secretary
Sandra Rhodes	Sales Administrative Assistant
Lila Lee	Assistant to the Director
Ruth Cooper	Receptionist

Creative Ideas for Household Storage is a Consumer Reports Book published by Consumers Union, the nonprofit organization that publishes *Consumer Reports,* the monthly magazine of test reports, product Ratings, and buying guidance. Established in 1936, Consumers Union is chartered under the Not-For-Profit Corporation Law of the State of New York.

The purposes of Consumers Union, as stated in its charter, are to provide consumers with information and counsel on consumer goods and services, to give information on all matters relating to the expenditure of the family income, and to initiate and to cooperate with individual and group efforts seeking to create and maintain decent living standards.

Consumers Union derives its income solely from the sale of *Consumer Reports* and other publications. In addition, expenses of occasional public service efforts may be met, in part, by nonrestrictive, non-commercial contributions, grants, and fees. Consumers Union accepts no advertising or product samples and is not beholden in any way to any commercial interest. Its Ratings and reports are solely for the use of the readers of its publications. Neither the Ratings nor the reports nor any Consumers Union publications, including this book, may be used in advertising or for any commercial purpose. Consumers Union will take all steps open to it to prevent such uses of its materials, its name, or the name of *Consumer Reports.*

Contents

Part II.   Storage Projects

Introduction

Almost everyone needs more storage space. Life-styles vary greatly from one era to another and from one family to another, but the layout of a house tends to remain fixed. After a move, during spring cleaning, or when lives change with the arrival of a new baby, householders often ask themselves, "Where can I put everything?" Most of us tend to accumulate more and more possessions; whether we live in an apartment, a condo, a co-op, or a house, there never seems to be enough room for them all. Moreover, as houses and apartments are downsized, people often have to fit more and more "goods and chattels" into less and less space. This book will help you do just that.

Nearly every living space, if organized properly, will conveniently hold more than may be apparent immediately. *Creative Ideas for Household Storage* emphasizes the principles of good storage:

1. Good storage is organized. It eliminates clutter and brings related items together.
2. Good storage is convenient. It is as close to the point of use as possible.
3. Good storage is expandable and adaptable. If you have something, it's almost certain you'll acquire more of it—books are a classic example. Your needs change; an elaborate cupboard for a stroller is a good idea only if it can be adapted to baseball gear and schoolbooks.

4. Good storage is divisible, to keep itself neat. It does not simply pile one object on top of another.
5. Good storage is individual. It is suited to the life-styles of those for whom it was developed.

Creative Ideas for Household Storage takes these principles into consideration while focusing on the house, room by room. Each chapter concerns itself with a particular living space, exploring the potential for storage units—closets, cabinets, drawers, racks, and shelves—suited to the activity of that specific area. In the bedroom, for example, we consider where and how our clothes can be housed most efficiently, where bed linen can be stored conveniently, and even how sleeping arrangements can be accommodated better. This involves describing closets—their interior shelving, racks, and special storage arrangements—chests, built-ins, and under-bed storage, as well as information on how best to provide bunk beds or a fold-out bed.

Creative Ideas for Household Storage looks first at what can or should be stored safely and conveniently in each room. Then we consider possible reorganization of the storage space in the room. Finally, we suggest modifications and additions that the average householder might take on.

Although some of the larger projects require a certain amount of do-it-yourself skill, most of the information is designed to be useful even to those who rarely take hammer in hand. Knowing what can be done is often as helpful as knowing how to do it yourself.

PART 1
Making and Using Space

1

THE LIVING ROOM

Of all the rooms in the house, the living room has the most varied uses and thus the most variety in what you want to store in it. Unlike the kitchen or the bedroom, whose names practically define their use, the living room no longer has a single function. It now substitutes for several rooms in the houses of an earlier time.

Our grandparents were used to keeping a back parlor, a front parlor, and a best room that was also called a drawing room. Day-to-day living took place in the back parlor. The best room was reserved for formal occasions; it was the showpiece of the house, where guests were received and entertained. Today, these functions are often combined in the living room, or in a separate family room—an informal gathering place where everyone relaxes and entertains. (Most of the storage solutions discussed in this chapter can apply equally well to separate family rooms.)

Furthermore, whereas many families manage to provide separate bedrooms for their children, large nurseries and playrooms are for most people a thing of the past. The living room must therefore also accommodate many childhood activities, which of course change as children grow.

Today's living room is thus, for many of us, a combination parlor, drawing room, library, TV-entertainment room, and playroom. Usually that will call for sofas, settees, and chairs of various descriptions and in various combinations, with side or coffee tables, perhaps a TV set, and a bookshelf or two. Then, to satisfy individual life-styles, add specialized storage, such as cabinets to house intricate hi-fi components or to display collections of all types.

There is, in short, no "typical" living room. The discussion that follows, therefore, is as comprehensive as possible so that each person can find solutions to the storage problems presented by his or her life-style. You can combine the elements in many ways; no two solutions are likely to be identical.

Whatever else goes on in the living room, it is primarily a place for your own personal comfort and relaxation. Besides providing you with a comfortable place to sit, the whole environment should be pleasant and relaxing. Whatever style you choose for it will work most effectively when storage solutions are given the same consideration as the color scheme and the choice of furnishings.

Most of us want more than a comfortable seat in an empty room. We do other things while sitting: we watch television, listen to music, read, knit, or tend to our collections. We also entertain, casually or formally. All of these activities involve paraphernalia that must be integrated successfully into the room's overall plan. Where and how these various objects are kept will depend not only on their size but on how accessible they need to be.

Beyond these considerations, the physical constraints of the room itself may well play an important role in deciding how things are arranged. When planning extra storage for any of the items or groups of items discussed in this chapter, keep in mind that although the accessibility of the stored item is important, the other roles of the room must be taken into account. Traffic patterns, for example, must be maintained; don't construct large shelving units where they'll have to be bypassed every time you want to cross the room. Similarly, keeping books and a comfortable chair near a light source makes more sense than storing the books around a TV set, which in use calls for more subdued lighting.

READING MATERIALS

A living room with no reading material of any kind is extremely rare. A few fortunate homeowners have a separate room they can use as a library. The rest of us will almost certainly have, at the least, a magazine or two, a few books, and probably a television program guide. Many people have a lot more.

Where you keep these books and magazines depends mainly on their number. If there are only a few, they may be kept conveniently on the almost universal coffee table. This is invariably close to the seating in which they will be read. Once the number exceeds more than a few, however, you need some special accommodation, which can range from a simple shelf or rack to a wall system.

Coffee Tables and Magazine Racks

When books and magazines are kept on a coffee table, they frequently need to be removed to make way for such things as the occasional snack (perhaps the very coffee for which the table is named). This can be something of a nuisance. While the possible shapes and sizes of coffee tables (and other tables) are virtually infinite, the most useful table is one that incorporates more than a single surface. This creates space for storage and display, leaving areas clear for serving or other purposes. Perhaps the simplest design is a table with a shelf below the top surface. If this top surface is glass, items can be displayed on the shelf below without interfering with the usable space on top (see figure 1.1).

Another way to accomplish the same end is to use other low storage forms as coffee tables. A whole range of cubes, boxes, and chests, often fitted with drawers, can be used as coffee tables. Since they come in a variety of styles,

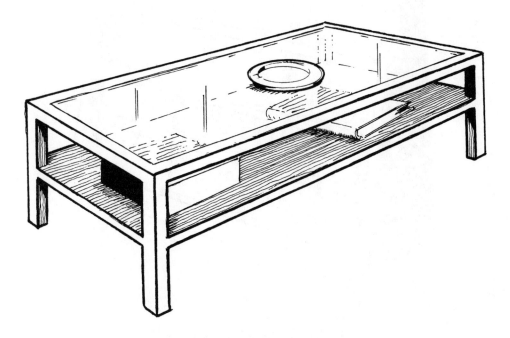

Figure 1.1 Glass-topped coffee table with shelf for books and magazines

they can be chosen to complement the seating arrangements and the decorating style of the room.

Almost all of us read magazines. Sometimes we get so swamped that it's hard to keep up, even with those we subscribe to. Yet it's hard to throw out unread magazines. They tend to accumulate in piles, at first on coffee tables and then in corners. Some form of systematized storage can bring these under control. It's not hard to keep a few magazines on the coffee table, but for any more than that it would be far better to have an open magazine rack, in which multiple copies are held and displayed without obscuring one other (see figure 1.2).

If you want to keep magazines as a reference library, you should consider more permanent shelf space. However, if they are too difficult to see or to get at, their usefulness as reference material will be seriously diminished. So shelf space alone is not always the best idea—numerous flimsy magazines stacked together are very unstable and difficult to deal with. Frequent partitions are needed to keep them upright and accessible. A practical alternative

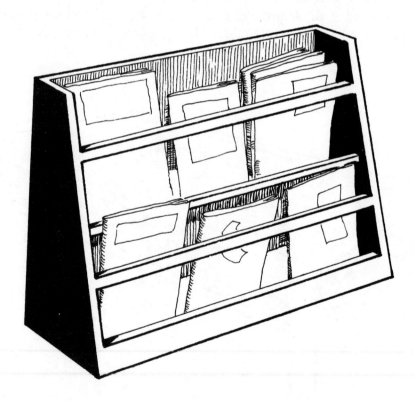

Figure 1.2   Open magazine rack

is the use of special binders or specially designed bins that hold a certain number of issues. Many publishers offer such binders or bins; also, variously sized self-assembling units, made of plastic or cardboard, often attractively decorated, can be found in most office and art-supply stores (see figure 1.3).

Larger periodicals and newspapers pose a different problem. While a few old newspapers can be extremely useful for general kitchen and household use, few of us need to keep every day's paper. Storage is not as great a problem as disposal, but one idea that can tidy up a household where many papers are read by many people is the use of café rods. These are no more than thin sticks of wood as long as the paper. They clip over the back of the paper, holding it firmly unfolded to its whole length while keeping the various pages from falling out.

Bookshelves and Bookcases

The simplest method of storing books in an accessible fashion is to use a pair of bookends. These can turn any flat surface, even one not designed for books, into a small library. A single bookend can serve if there is a convenient solid upright (such as a wall) to substitute for the other end. Bookends come in a variety of styles from plain library-style metal types to more ornamental designs.

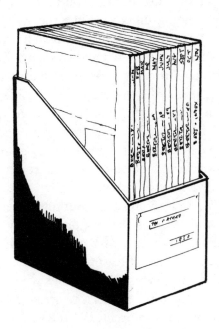

Figure 1.3 Magazine bin

Slightly more adventurous is the use of small book racks designed to hold a dozen books or more. These too can be located on any available flat surface.

At the other end of the scale are full-fledged bookcases. Their size and degree of complexity are virtually unlimited. It is easy to decide you need a bookcase; what you must keep in mind is that a bookcase is a piece of furniture requiring the same kind of consideration in design and placement as other large pieces, such as sofas and tables. Project 1 (see page 103) describes the building of a basic bookcase.

Between the simple pair of bookends and the complete bookcase exists an endless array of shelving and built-in units you can choose to fit the number of books you need (or want) to keep readily at hand. The possibilities range from simple boards resting on blocks or boxes to sophisticated modular units found in home-furnishing stores. But before buying the first freestanding unit that appeals to you, examine the physical layout of the room carefully.

Many living rooms have fireplaces with projecting chimney breasts. The recessed bays at either side of the chimney, if not already fitted with shelves or cupboards, form ideal locations for storage units of many different types. If it's shelves you want, these need not be wall-to-wall wood cases built into their own frames; shelving supported by a wall-mounted standard-and-bracket system may be perfectly adequate. Similar recessed spaces may become apparent once you start thinking along these lines.

No matter what type of book storage you plan, adjustable shelving is a great advantage. Freestanding units that line the walls or clearly serve as room dividers should be adjustable whenever possible; you never know when you may want to change their contents and configuration. However, rather than adding a succession of different, possibly ill-matched, freestanding units as your library grows, it may be preferable to consider built-ins that take advantage of the shape of the room. Much can be done to improve the looks of an awkwardly designed room by "tying together" odd windows or doors with a continuous line of shelving. If there is simply no room for floor-based cases, you can sometimes run a shelf around the room at the height of the door tops to hold an overflow of books.

There are, in extremes, more unusual solutions: The back of a door can be lined with shelves, which might well disguise a rarely used opening; space might be found inside an existing closet or cupboard; or books might be stored in the once-popular piece of furniture known as a library table.

Another solution for the devoted bibliophile who simply doesn't have enough wall space for all his or her books is to arrange shelves perpendicular to the wall, projecting out into the center of the room. This need not be as clumsy as it may at first sound, especially if the shelving is constructed to take advantage of sloping or irregularly shaped walls.

ENTERTAINMENT SYSTEMS

The list of audio and video components grows longer each year. At first there was only a gramophone (the ancestor of today's record player); then came the radio and the TV set. Now the list includes a tape deck, a compact disc player, a videocassette recorder, and such hi-fi components as an amplifier, a preamplifier, a tuner, and speakers. Finally, there are all the collected tape reels, audiocassettes, records, compact discs, and videocassettes to play on these systems.

As each of these components made its appearance in our living rooms, it was usually housed in a separate, proudly displayed cabinet, the equal of any other piece of furniture in the room. The integration of these diverse systems was slow but inevitable, and now the so-called entertainment center, containing all or most of these components, is common.

Nevertheless, since most of us have accumulated this equipment over a period of time, we still face the problem of deciding where and how to group the units most efficiently or to disperse them around the room.

The Television Set

The TV set is waging a largely successful battle with the fireplace as the focal point of the living room. But in homes where fireplaces still exist and are used, the TV set has often compromised by becoming mobile. Special stands or carts for the TV set have become common. They often have space for the VCR and its accompanying cassettes, and possibly a shelf for program guides and magazines (see figure 1.4). A drawback with this system is that sooner or later the cassette collection overflows the television cart and additional shelving becomes necessary.

It is obviously important to locate the television where it can be seen most comfortably from the seating arrangements. Building the television set into a fixed location, such as a wall unit, is often the most efficient way to create space and store all the attendant paraphernalia, but since rooms are rearranged from time to time, this must be thought out carefully.

Many TV sets are substantial objects—and not the most attractive ones— so putting them inside a cabinet, perhaps on a swiveling slide-out shelf, is an idea you may want to consider. Though TV sets are not nearly as deep as they once were, they are still deeper than most objects on the usual shelf.

Bear in mind that television sets, and hi-fi components as well, require ventilation around them so that they don't overheat. Check the owner's manual for the manufacturer's recommendations.

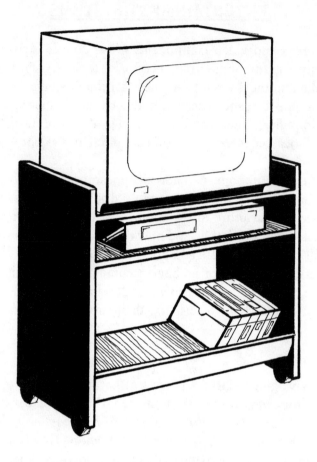

Figure 1.4   Television and videocassette recorder cart

Other Components

Similarly, although perhaps to a slightly lesser extent, you should locate the other entertainment systems where they can be operated easily. At the same time, you should consider where and how the record, disc, and tape collections can be housed—they need to be nearby and accessible. (Keep in mind that LP records are 12-inch squares and will not fit well in a standard bookcase.) Apart from accessibility the most important thing is to allow for possible expansion, certainly of collections and possibly of components. If this has been considered, designated cabinets, whether known as stereo cabinets, entertainment units, or whatever, can be the best solution. If this is not possible, small units for keeping collections of tapes and discs are readily available (see figure 1.5). These can often be tucked into a variety of areas too small for an entire system. When choosing a place to house collections

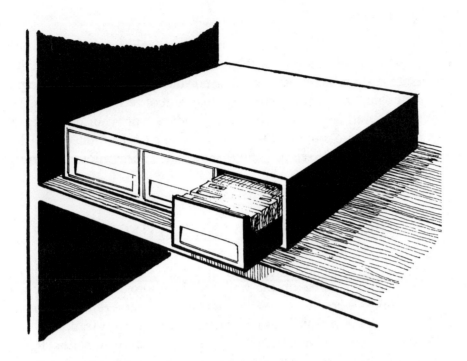

Figure 1.5   Three-drawer audiocassette storage unit

of tapes and discs, try to avoid areas with excessive heat and light, such as on top of radiators or heat vents, or near windows.

In some circumstances, it may be possible to incorporate one or more of your systems into existing shelving or cabinets, with books and other items. Some of the solutions suggested for book and magazine storage may be applicable here as well.

Just as the TV screen may dictate its location, so too may speakers dictate their location. The need for proper viewing plus the desire for good acoustics may well determine the layout of the rest of the room. Some speaker systems are designed to be freestanding units, but others can be wall mounted or incorporated into shelving or cabinetry. As noted, the decision may turn on performance considerations.

Once you have decided roughly where and how the entertainment equipment will be placed, consider how you will bring the necessary wiring to all the electronic components. It would be best to plan sufficiently far ahead so that all the required outlets and interfaces are safely and discreetly built in. Even so, you have to allow for wires to reach the outlets and, often, the other components.

Bringing It Together

Although there are a variety of factory-made stereo cabinets designed to hold a variety of components, often with shelf space for records and tapes, it is often best to custom-build such a cabinet, so you can provide for a changing selection of components and a growing collection of records and tapes. The possible configurations of such built-ins are endless; your choice will depend on what you want to store and the physical shape of the room in which it is to be built. Project 2 (see page 109) shows the construction of a typical entertainment unit.

COLLECTIONS, SOUVENIRS, AND GAMES

This category includes practically everything else you might find in a living room. Beyond the pictures on the wall and the photographs on the piano or mantel, almost every living room holds some mementos of the occupants' lives. These can range from seashells picked up during a vacation to souvenirs—china, figurines, or unusual objects—from faraway places. It may just be a group of pretty objects the owner likes to have around. A few such mementos do not usually present a display or storage problem, but when they accumulate over a lifetime they're another matter. When shelves are filled to overflowing and every surface crammed with assorted knickknacks, some better plan is called for.

Specific collections are somewhat different; they frequently require specialized housing right from the start. Stamps call for albums; coins need drawers, as do butterfly collections, medals, and other fragile objects. Larger items, such as china plates, usually require cabinets of some kind to house and display them safely.

The key to successful storage of special objects is to be realistic about the extent of your collecting mania. Once you go beyond just a few things, it is better to dedicate a special storage and display area specifically suited to whatever you're collecting.

Shelving and Wall Units

The obvious first choice is a set of wall shelves put up expressly to hold particular items. These can be simply made and tailored to make the best use of the available space. Project 3 (see page 113) shows a basic display shelf that can be adapted in many ways.

Another solution is to allot the collection a special area in a cabinet that already exists in the room, one or two compartments in a wall unit or shelving unit, for example. Doing this often draws interest to the cabinet itself and can make better use of space otherwise going to waste. This may mean adding smaller shelves or cabinets within the whole.

It should be remembered that "wall units" is a term that comprises an enormous range of designs. Constructing a wall full of simple shelving constitutes a wall unit just as much as does providing a complicated system of adjustable shelves, drawers, partitions, cabinet doors, and pull-down desktops. Almost anything you might want to store can be accommodated in a wall unit, if specially designed, and a wall unit can be designed for virtually any wall space no matter what shape or size.

Note that "wall" units need not line a wall. A freestanding wall unit is often a legitimate choice for a room divider. Similarly, a wall unit need not rest on the floor; units designed to be mounted on a wall above a radiator, for example, often prove an apt solution.

Also popular and particularly practical for delicate and special items is the display or curio cabinet. Because of its doors and drawer space, such a piece protects its contents far better than free storage in an open wall unit. Often the doors are made of glass for better display. If it incorporates its own lighting, the piece can become an attractive focal point as well as an efficient storage unit.

Earlier we discussed the use of coffee tables with shelves or drawer space. Other tables can also have drawers, providing an ideal location for games and game equipment—such as chess sets, checker pieces, playing cards, and board games.

HIDDEN OBJECTS

There are certain items useful in a living room that you do not necessarily want on display, such as cleaning equipment, hobby supplies, firewood, or extra cushions. For such things you should consider closed cabinets, shelf space with fitted doors, or chests that can be used as coffee tables, wall seats, or simply as pieces of furniture in their own right. Hideaway storage can also be found in window seats and occasionally in areas over closets. There is, too, the odd nook, sometimes designed into corners, or by fireplaces, or that is a result of other architectural features (around staircases, for example).

Storage space can be created in many of these locations, built and decorated to merge with the room's basic construction by being painted or papered to match the rest of the room. Project 4 (see page 117) shows how to build a typical window seat.

2

THE DINING ROOM

As space becomes more and more at a premium in today's shrinking house, the separate dining room becomes more and more of a luxury. It still exists, of course, in older houses and in large new houses, but it is almost more common today to find either a dual-purpose room or a separate area within an existing room.

Sometimes, an area of the living room is reserved for eating, with a permanent table used for day-to-day activities, then cleared for dining. In other cases, the dining room shares space with an office, a study, or even a library— all providing quiet alternatives to the everyday activities of the living room.

Even more common, perhaps, is to set aside a special area of another room to be used solely for eating. This is not a new idea. Many older houses have large rooms that can be divided by the use of folding screens or doors, to provide a separate dining area when needed. A more recent approach, however, has been to make the kitchen larger and use part of the extra space as an eating area.

Today's kitchens frequently provide counter areas or table space at which meals may be prepared and eaten. (For a fuller discussion of eating spaces in the kitchen itself, see chapter 5.) It is a small and logical step from such a design to one that provides a separate dining area on the other side of a counter-height divider, or peninsula, as it is sometimes called.

Even in houses with a true separate dining room, in today's world it makes sense to provide some sort of informal eating space, such as a breakfast nook perhaps, in or adjoining the kitchen.

DINING AREAS

A dining area, as opposed to a dedicated dining room, has many advantages. Apart from the obvious benefit of preparing food and consuming it in adjacent areas, the person cooking can stay in better social contact with family and/or guests. Small children, for example, might be at risk in a busy kitchen but can easily be supervised in an eating area nearby. The divider that often separates the two areas itself becomes an integral part of the cooking and dining process: it provides both work space and storage for the numerous items of equipment and tableware needed on a continual basis.

Beneath its countertop, for example, the divider can house a major appliance such as a dishwasher or a variety of cabinets and shelves needed for kitchen storage. The divider is the perfect place to store items that are used both in the kitchen and the living room. Dishes, glassware, and silverware can be stored here in such a way that they can be reached from both sides— used for dining when needed, then stored after being washed in the kitchen.

If part of the divider's top surface is made higher than normal working counter height, 42 inches rather than 34 to 36 inches, it can be used as an eating counter at which stools may be placed. Where space is at a premium, part of this eating counter can be a fold-down flap that can be lowered out of the way when not in use. A counter-high cabinet can be used in conjunction with a ceiling-hung unit, leaving a pass-through between. The divider, however, need not be a full-fledged built-in. It can be a set of open shelves or nothing more than a rod from which a divider of baskets or pots is hung.

The divider may well function as a bar, complete with a small sink if desired, with the counter for making drinks and the cabinets for storing glasses, as well as other items, either below the counter or overhead.

SEATING AND TABLEWARE

Whatever else may be needed where you eat, somewhere to sit and something to sit at are of the first order of importance.

Given unlimited space, a large dining table seating ten or more might be appropriate. Yet even where this is feasible, the table might prove to be formidable for a lone diner or a couple. If there is any extra space at all, the best table is one that can be expanded and contracted to fit different occasions.

Such tables are adapted to changing conditions in a variety of ways. The simplest is just putting together two separate units. When not needed, one can be stored against the wall. Another solution is the use of tables fitted with drop leaves that can be folded up or down as required. Tables with self-storing leaves, which rest under the main top until required, have been used for centuries. There are also many types of expanding tables, which may be drawn apart, allowing other parts to pop up or unfold in ingenious ways. Probably the commonest design, however, is an extension table to which extra leaves (stored elsewhere) can be added, usually at the center of the table, resting on the expanding table framework while it is opened.

Such extension tables are made in many basic shapes, but if the idea is to go from the smallest possible surface area to the largest, the circular table (without its leaves) accomplishes that best.

The particular shape of a dining area, however, may not allow a circular table as easily as a rectangular one, which can be placed close to or against a wall. Then again, more places can be set around a given circumference if it's round than if it's interrupted by corners. In either case, you must find a place to store the leaves when they're not being used (see "Linens and Miscellaneous Items" later in this chapter).

In choosing the most efficient table for your particular space, other things besides simply the number of expected diners must be considered.

The most practical solution, for example, might be to do without a permanent table altogether. Instead, you might use a counter space or a fold-down flap as an eating surface. Or perhaps you have room for a booth or banquette arrangement around a table that is permanently attached at one end to a wall.

Seating and Potential Storage

There may not be much storage potential in the average dining-room chair, but there *are* ways to provide seating and extra storage at the same time. We've already suggested the use of stools at a counter for situations where there is little room for a separate table. This is an extreme case, of course, and there are other, less drastic solutions. One is to make use of benches instead of individual chairs, at least on one side of the table. If these benches are made like a box, with hinged tops, a surprising amount of storage space will be created. Since such storage benches can become heavy, it is probably practical to use them only when the benches can be placed along a wall, perhaps attached to it. Project 4 (see page 117) shows how to build a window seat that can serve as a wall bench.

An old-fashioned settle (see figure 2.1), which was originally designed to protect the occupant from chill drafts from behind when sitting at the fire, provides another option. It can be used at a table, thus providing plenty of space beneath the seat to keep all manner of things. If the settle is located at right angles to the wall, it can function much like a booth, adding privacy or defining the area.

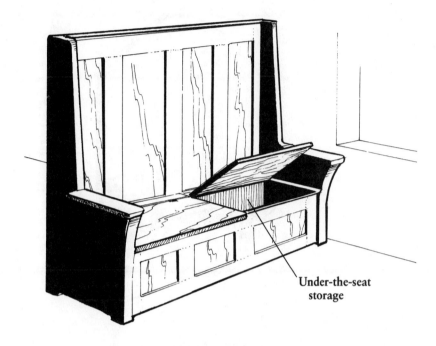

Under-the-seat
storage

Figure 2.1   Traditional wooden settle

As a last resort, if you have absolutely no space for permanent seating, with or without storage, it is always possible to use folding chairs. These, of course, require their own storage space.

Dishes

Although dishes can be stored elsewhere, it is often very appropriate to store—if not display—your plates, cups and saucers, and other dishes in the dining room or dining area.

The simplest and most direct way to do this is to hang the dishes on the wall. While this is usually reserved for collections or for antique dishes, there is no reason why attractive arrangements cannot be made of other good-looking modern items, especially if space in cabinets or on shelves is at a premium. Another approach is to use special wall-hung shelves designed to hold plates or platters upright; these are made with a shallow groove that holds the edge of each dish (see figure 2.2). Taken to extremes, this idea involves a continuous shelf running around the wall at or above head height, a solution often found in old inns and taverns. This technique may also be used to display smaller items, such as a collection of pretty cups and saucers.

You can achieve much more display space, however, with a freestanding china cabinet (or cabinets). Such a cabinet can often hold complete services

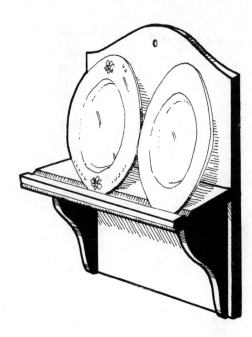

Figure 2.2   Grooved dish rack

of plates, platters, cups and saucers, tureens, and other dishes, arranged so that they are displayed to advantage.

Related to the china cabinet is the sideboard, once common in kitchens but now more often a handsome addition to a dining room or area. The sideboard was originally designed as a working space, with open shelves above and closed cabinets below. The upper shelves, invariably grooved to hold dishes upright, can be adapted, with the addition of hooks, to hang items with handles, such as cups and jugs. The cabinets below are ideal for bulk storage of stacks of dishes not worth displaying.

Yet another freestanding solution to dish storage in a dining area is the use of a cabinet not specifically designed for dishes. Any piece of closable furniture that goes well with the room can be used as is or fitted out for china storage. Antique armoires and rehabilitated record cabinets, to name two examples, can hold surprising quantities of china, especially if shelving and racks are provided inside to accommodate your particular requirements.

Built-in storage.   One advantage of built-in storage is that it can easily be customized to fit your particular needs. If island cabinets or closets or other built-in cabinets are designed specifically for dining-room storage, the space inside can be put to work most efficiently. As we mentioned earlier, a storage divider that can be accessed from two sides, one with doors on the dining side and the kitchen side, is often very convenient. The shelving should be so arranged as to make this as useful as possible by installing sliding shelves or trays that can be pulled out from either side, or revolving racks.

In any event, dishes should never be stacked in excessively high piles. Not only is this dangerous, but you invariably discover that the pattern you want is at the bottom of the heap. In planning a new cabinet, it's far better to design a system of closely spaced shelving. In existing cabinets, fit freestanding racks over your stacks of dishes. These are either wood or plastic-coated metal racks, which can both be found in houseware stores and in department stores.

Not everybody lives in areas prone to earthquakes, but those who do are well advised to store dishes and other breakables in cupboards that can be securely closed, with a mechanical latch rather than a magnetic catch that might be bounced open. If feasible, locate dish storage so that the doors to these cupboards or cabinets are perpendicular to the fault zone. Shock waves emanating from these zones will then rock the contents only sideways rather than spilling them out the front of the cabinets.

Cutlery

Cutlery as used here is meant to include flatware and serving utensils as well as knives and other cutting instruments. Special sets are often best kept in the velvet-lined boxes they are sold in; they make handsome display items on their own account. Another traditional container is the knife box, sometimes fashioned in the shape of an urn. It was designed to be an ornament and is often placed on the dining table or sideboard.

More common today, however, is the compartmentalized drawer or bin to separate knives, forks, and spoons. Although these are often found in the kitchen, near the sink or dishwasher, there is no reason why they cannot be in the dining area—under tables or in cabinets or closets. It is a simple matter to add partitions to an existing drawer, either self-made or ones chosen from the many dividers available commercially. (See project 5, page 123.)

If the dining area is separated from the kitchen by a counter or divider, storing cutlery in containers on the counter itself is extremely convenient, if you can spare the counter space. If not, consider using cloth or net slings suspended below the upper cabinets (see figure 2.3).

For other ideas on cutlery storage, see Chapter 5, "The Kitchen."

Glassware

Also appropriate for storage in the dining room is glassware, especially quality stemware that should be kept out of the hurly-burly of the kitchen.

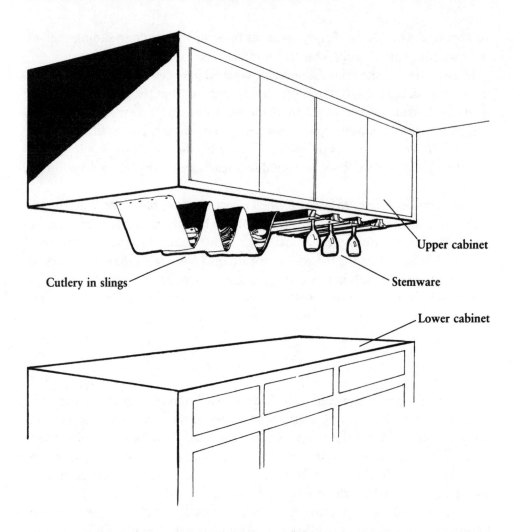

Cutlery in slings

Upper cabinet

Stemware

Lower cabinet

Figure 2.3   Cutlery slings and stemware rack

This category also includes glass items such as serving plates, bowls, pitchers, and vases. These are frequently kept on display in the dining room.

Even if you aren't displaying the glassware, it may still make sense to keep stemware in the dining room, either in its own cabinet or in a compartment of a larger cabinet. It may be possible to build special racks or shelves into existing cabinets. A glass-fronted cabinet, whether as part of a major sideboard or wall-hung by itself, can be very attractive in a dining room. It can sometimes be located so as to use the reflective quality of the glass to good effect in an otherwise dark corner. A dining-area divider that has an upper section provides an excellent place from which to hang bar-type racks: stemmed glasses are hung upside down supported by their bases, held between wooden slats (see figure 2.3). They are not only quickly accessible but also out of the way and thus relatively safe.

Linens and Miscellaneous Items

There are various other appurtenances of both formal and casual dining that are normally kept in the dining room, small items such as napkin rings and trivets, linens such as tablecloths and place mats, and even large items such as cake stands and chafing dishes. Many of these items are light and flat, and consequently well adapted to being kept in the kind of shallow drawer that might be easily fitted under tabletops or in otherwise unused areas of cabinets. Shallow drawers with extra low fronts, such as those often found in a traditional sideboard, make selection of table linens especially easy.

Sideways storage, in narrow areas such as the space between cabinets, is a convenient way to keep extra leaves for an extension table, folding chairs, and similar large but narrow objects. Fitting out a space in a closet so that these items can be held and removed individually makes their use far more convenient, since you rarely use all of them at once. Of course, extra table leaves sometimes come in their own chest or cabinet; if not too ugly, this cabinet can often double as extra chest-type seating rather than being consigned to the attic or basement.

FOOD AND DRINK

There is not much food apart from bowls of fruit and nuts that can be stored for any period of time in a dining area, but food is many times served in the dining room. The necessary serving pieces—hutches, buffets, sideboards—can also be used as storage areas for many of the items already mentioned. Several of these pieces, in fact, commonly contain drawers and shelves expressly designed to hold dining equipment that cannot be fitted in anywhere else. Chafing dishes and cake stands, mentioned before, are typical examples of the kind of awkward item that does not really fit the typical storage cabinet easily. Often, it is easy to update these older pieces by simply adding extra shelves or drawers; they can then hold a wealth of things that might otherwise clutter up space needed for items in constant use.

A serving cart is another common item in dining areas. Fitted with casters and used for transporting food and drink to and from the kitchen, serving carts often have space as well for tableware, such as napkins, candlesticks, and fruit bowls. More elaborate carts have drawers for cutlery, racks for glasses, even racks for spices and bottles of sauces. Project 6 shows a simple serving cart (see page 126).

Under the heading of drink may be a full-fledged bar with a complete wine cellar, or simply a shelf or counter to hold a couple of bottles. Wine lovers will want to dedicate a whole wall to wine racks; there is almost no limit to the storage options for wine bottles. These range from simple bins made from lengths of tubular material (cardboard, plastic, or even ceramic) to commercial racks arranged in self-stacking units or built into shelving.

The prime consideration when storing wine is proper temperature control. Few homes today can afford the luxury of an underground wine cellar, but there may be other areas of the house where the temperature does not change radically from hot to cold. Because it's not in constant use, a dining room may well be one of those areas. Wherever you keep wines, however, avoid proximity to radiators, heating vents, and stoves and fireplaces; try to avoid drafty areas near doorways or windows as well. A dark place away from direct sunlight and insulated from excessive vibration—from dishwashers or other household machinery—is also suggested.

In a small house, the dining area is the logical place for a small bar. Beyond storage space for liquor and glassware, it might well hold related items such as bowls and small dishes for snacks to have with drinks. If there is not enough room for a totally separate bar, it may still be possible to use part of a divider, or even convert part of an existing cabinet or closet, perhaps with a fold-out serving counter.

BEYOND FOOD AND DINING

Finally, the dining room or dining area may be the place to keep, store, or even display other things—potted plants, African sculpture, fine editions, what-have-you—for which there is simply no other place in the house. How and where these can be dealt with is largely a matter of what they are and how much space there is, but the important thing is to remember that the dining-room option exists—for almost anything. If included within the overall design format of the room, quite unexpected items might find a felicitous home.

3

THE BEDROOM

The average person spends almost a third of his or her life asleep. As a result, we tend to think of the bedroom—the room in which we spend more time than we do in any other—primarily in terms of the bed itself. While the bed is certainly a large piece of furniture and can easily dominate the room, for many, the bedroom also serves other purposes—to relax, to watch television, to read a little before falling asleep. Perhaps most important for storage considerations, however, the bedroom is where we keep our clothes and dress ourselves. Few people these days can afford the luxury of a separate dressing room.

While men may groom themselves mainly in the bathroom, many women prefer the comfort of their bedroom to fix their hair and apply makeup. The bedroom is thus, for many women, a "boudoir."

A bedroom may occasionally become a sickroom, a place not so much to sleep as to rest and recuperate. A spare bedroom, which is occupied from time to time by guests, is similarly only partly intended for sleeping, since it must also serve as the guest's private living room.

The nursery, as such, has almost disappeared from the average house. Children's bedrooms, these days referred to simply as so-and-so's room, are de facto nurseries, playrooms, and study rooms, and consequently must be designed for many more activities than simply sleeping.

It is obvious, therefore, that we need far more in a bedroom than just a bed. The room needs to be very carefully planned if it is to fulfill all of the required functions satisfactorily and not disappear under a welter of clothes, linens, books, toys, toiletries, and other assorted items.

THE BED

As a starting point, we should consider the sleeping surface itself. There are many ways to provide such a surface besides the traditional bed. If space is severely limited, you might consider those to create more space and a better organized room. Even if you decide on a traditional bed, it can often be used as a storage device in its own right, apart from its primary function as a place to sleep.

Our ancestors were in many ways more practical than we've been. Except for the very wealthy, they often dispensed with a permanent bed altogether and slept in alcoves, on benches, or on simple pallets rolled out on the floor. By comparison, today's standard bed is an uncompromisingly large item. Beds in forms other than the traditional headboard, footboard, and mattress-supporting frame are increasingly common, however. Some of these are designed primarily to take up minimum space or to become as unobtrusive as possible, whereas others are specifically designed for purposes beyond merely sleeping.

Convertibles and Divans

Convertible beds that unfold from sofas and couches are so often so well designed today that one would never suspect them of concealing a comfortable bed. Of course, this is an arrangement more suited to the living room than a full-fledged bedroom, but when the bedroom has to serve for much daytime use or cannot easily hold a standard bed, a convertible may be the solution. It can also provide the occasional extra bed in an otherwise standard bedroom, allowing the luxury of its use as a sofa when not needed for guests.

The term convertible usually conjures up pictures of couches that unfold, revealing a more or less complicated system of framing and extra legs. Yet a simple divan (a couch without sides or back) can serve in the same way, its daytime slipcover being removed at night, allowing it to be made up as a bed.

A recent type of convertible bed, especially popular in temporary situations such as student housing, is the Japanese *futon*. The futon is a firm mat that can be folded out, either on the floor or on a simple wooden frame, thus serving either as a bed or a backed couch.

Trundle and Stowaway Beds

Another way to add sleeping space is the trundle bed. This is a low bed on wheels, designed to store under a standing bed. Although this design is very old—there are examples dating from the sixteenth century—modern metal versions are available. They're an excellent solution for the problem of occasional extra sleeping accommodation, especially in children's rooms.

There are other solutions to the problem of providing extra—often temporary—sleeping space in restricted areas, including hammocks, beds that fold down or out from walls, fold-up camp beds, collapsible cots, and the like.

The Murphy Bed

The Murphy bed, which folds completely away into the wall, was originally to be concealed behind doors but is now frequently designed so that the underside of the bed, when folded away, forms a continuous surface with the wall. It is named for its nineteenth-century inventor, William L. Murphy. The built-in version of the Murphy bed requires considerable planning and fairly sophisticated construction, but the cabinet version, which is attached to the wall and projects only about 18 inches into the room, is easily installed. Although more expensive than other foldaways, the Murphy bed does provide a dramatic way of storing a bed and creating a lot of space usable during the day.

Bunk, Loft, and Platform Beds

If your ceilings are high enough, there are other ways to free up the floor space by elevating the bed permanently onto a loft, a platform, or simply in the stacking arrangement known as a bunk bed.

A loft bed is created by building an additional floor, large enough to contain bedding, or even an entire bed, at or above head level. The advantage is that floor space is gained; the disadvantage is that you usually cannot stand up in the sleeping area, though it is perfectly adequate for sitting and sleeping. It is often an ideal solution for a growing family and need not be very complicated to construct. Project 7 (page 130) shows the construction details for a sleeping loft.

A platform bed is a related idea: the bed is located on top of another structure. It may be well off the floor, over a system of cabinets and shelves, high enough to require a ladder. Or it may be fairly low and situated within an alcove, perhaps under a window. If it's within an alcove, with storage space below, it's only a short step to closing the space off with doors. That creates a bed-size cubicle for the sleeper and effectively conceals the bed from the rest of the room (see figure 3.1).

Bunk beds are usually thought of as a double-decker, one directly over the other, but the bunk bed was originally created as a single bed for typical shipboard sleeping. Furthermore, it is not always necessary, or desirable, to position the two beds directly over one another; they may quite as easily be positioned at right angles, using the available space to better advantage (see figure 3.2). The lower bunk bed shown here is in many ways similar to the captain's bed described on pages 27–28.

The Bed as a Storage Unit

Unless the bedroom has to do double duty as a study or living room, most people will be content with a traditional bed. The bed has to be made every day, and alcove and bunk beds are notoriously hard to make. Nevertheless,

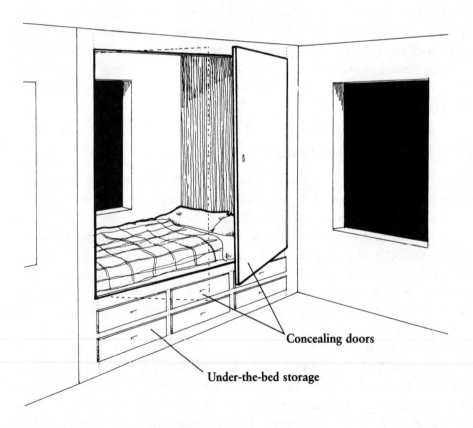

Concealing doors

Under-the-bed storage

Figure 3.1 Cabinet bed

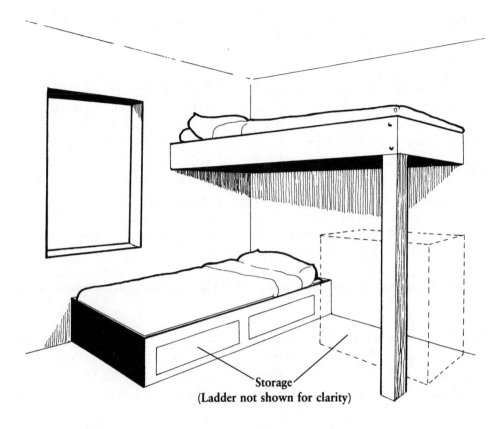

Storage
(Ladder not shown for clarity)

Figure 3.2   Unaligned bunk beds

there is no reason why the bed should utilize so much space for its single function. It can easily become an efficient and convenient storage unit in its own right.

To start with, there is that often wasted space beneath the bed. Instead of remaining a relatively inaccessible area that swallows up odd socks and produces endless dust balls, this space can be used in a variety of ways to store clothes, linens, or almost anything else.

Captain's bed. Very similar to a bunk bed at floor level, a captain's bed is simply an arrangement in which the mattress is supported not on a frame and legs but on a kind of boxed platform. The variations in design are endless. They include a box with drawers that pull out from one or both sides—or even from the ends—or a box with a dead storage area available only by lifting up the platform on which the mattress rests. A captain's bed with just two large drawers is ideally suited for keeping extra blankets and linens, whereas one with smaller drawers might be more suitable for keeping articles of clothing. Before buying or building such a bed, be sure you've settled on the bed's intended location, since unlike a traditional bed, its access must be left on the sides where drawers open.

Roll-out drawers. You can have under-bed storage, however, without giving up the traditional bed. Assuming the bed is high enough off the floor, roll-out trays or boxes can be fitted underneath. Although there are many commercially available under-bed trays and chests (made of plastic, cardboard, wood, or metal), it may be best to make your own. They can be designed specifically to fit *your* bed and *your* storage needs. In planning these, consider the following: accessibility (the container should be easy to reach and easy to roll out), partitioning (the container should be divided for better organization), and dust protection (some form of covering must keep out that dust). If the bed is far enough off the floor, and the roll-out provided with a flat lid, it can also serve as a temporary bedside table for the occasional drink or sandwich. See Project 8 (page 133) for a simple under-bed roll-out.

Other under-bed storage. Beds located on raised platforms, already mentioned, can be ideal places for storage. The interior of the platform can be accessed either by drawers or by cabinet doors. Loft beds can also have racks or cabinets added beneath them if there is sufficient headroom.

Storage Around the Bed

Not only can the space beneath a bed be put to good use, but the space all around the bed can become storage as well. Chests or boxes can be positioned simply adjacent to the bed—in the form of foot-of-the-bed chests, for example. Or the bed itself can rest on a captain's-bed-type base that is larger than the actual mattress, so the bed is surrounded on one or more sides with bins or chests. The tops of these can provide seating at the same height as the bed. The tops can lift up or there can be doors or drawers accessed from the outside. In planning such an installation, you must leave the bed sufficiently accessible for easy making. When storage units like these are upholstered or finished to match the room's decor, they can do much to enhance the room's attractiveness as well as provide a good place for bulky items like extra pillows and comforters.

Headboards and nightstands. Whether or not there is room to add low storage units around the bed, there will usually be room for a table or bedside cabinet of some sort next to the head of the bed. Almost everyone needs a lamp and an alarm clock, if not a place for books and other bedside impedimenta. It is not difficult to design an efficient nightstand fitted to your own personal needs.

A logical extension of the nightstand is to incorporate it into the headboard. Originally designed simply as a support when sitting up in bed and perhaps to protect the wall and prevent the pillows from falling off, the headboard is now often enlarged to become a virtual wall unit.

A headboard storage unit may consist simply of a large chest or bin extending across the top end of the bed. As such, it provides a comfortable place against which to rest as well as a framework that can be fitted out with shelves or cabinets. It can be made much wider than the bed, of course, and so perform the functions of a nightstand at one or both sides of the bed. It can also be built to extend above the bed, providing closed or open shelving for items likely to be needed when in bed—books, magazines, a telephone, and the like. Such an extensive headboard storage unit might form an appropriate surround for a Murphy bed.

A large storage headboard can also act as a room divider. It may not always be desirable to position a bed against a wall, and in a large room it might also be desirable to provide a degree of separation or privacy. A freestanding bed fitted with a large, almost wall-sized headboard satisfies both these demands. Indeed, it can create an actual dressing area if the headboard is positioned a few feet away from the wall. In this case, the headboard unit might be constructed in double depth so the back contains storage space—perhaps even a closet for clothes or a dressing mirror. The space created behind a large headboard unit can be ideal for locating any type of exercise machine.

LINENS AND BLANKETS

Next to the bed itself, probably the bulkiest storage needed in the bedroom is for what goes on the bed. Any or all of it—linens, blankets, comforters, quilts, and all—can be kept elsewhere in the house if necessary, but it's far more convenient to have them close at hand. As we've mentioned, it may well be possible to provide space for these items in chests, bins, or under-bed containers built especially for the purpose in the bedroom itself.

There's not much that can be done with large quilts and similar bulky items except to store them folded, in a well-aired and mothproof location. But there are other ways to keep blankets. Consider a system of rods, arranged much like towel racks, attached to the back of a closet door; individual blankets can be draped over the rods, overlapping just enough so some of each blanket remains visible (see figure 3.3).

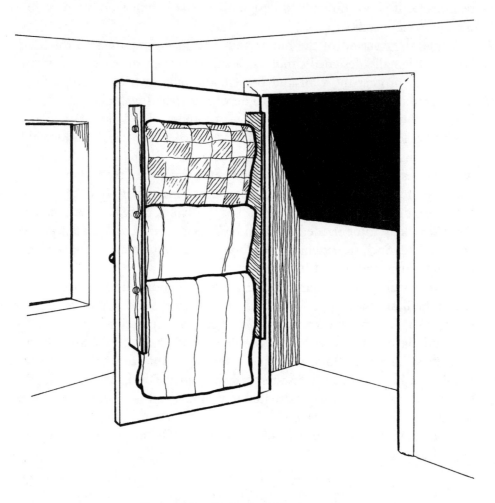

Figure 3.3   Closet-door blanket rack

THE CLOSET

We have already touched on the possibility of keeping some articles of clothing in storage built against or around the bed. But no matter how much of this space you can create, there will still be a need for a dedicated clothes area. The wardrobe, a roomy, self-contained cabinet with drawers and hanging space, used to serve this purpose. The French term *armoire* refers to a similar piece of furniture, particularly an antique. Today, most bedrooms include built-in closet space intended specifically for clothing. In fact, in many building codes, it is the presence of a built-in closet that defines a room as a bedroom.

Nevertheless, most closets in older homes, and also in today's development houses, leave much to be desired. The builder typically fits them out with one continuous hanging rod and a single shelf with much too much space above it. This bare-bones arrangement wastes space and encourages clutter and confusion. There is often unused space on the shelf above the closet rod, and the rod itself is usually both too low for long items—which then trail on the floor—and at the same time so high that many shorter items, like shirts and jackets, leave much empty space below them.

With a little thought, you can do much to dramatically improve the capacity and efficiency of the average closet. Instead of one rod at the standard 64-inch height, most closets work much better if they're fitted out with rods at two or more heights, positioned to accommodate clothes of a particular length. No space will be wasted above or below the rods; furthermore, shorter rods will carry more weight without sagging (see figure 3.4).

In reworking a closet, be sure to get the shoes off the floor. There is never enough room for them there, they endanger clothes that hang full length, and they make it difficult to clean the closet floor. Install racks or a system of shoe-size cubbyholes (see figure 3.5), or hang a pocket system behind a door.

Between the now shorter rods fixed at different heights, you can create stacks of shelving to hold everything from sweaters to shoes. The more shelves there are, the better you'll be able to separate out small groups of similar items.

This shelving can be created in various ways: wood shelves can be built or bought; there are also modular basket systems that are particularly suited to certain items. The basket systems are easily installed; the baskets generally slide in and out, though you can see the contents even when closed.

Instead of stacks of shelves, consider chests of drawers, which often can be accommodated inside a closet. If they're high enough, they can serve as partitions within the closet, supporting the closet rods.

There are, of course, complete packaged systems for transforming the standard closet into an efficient storage space. They include many accessories designed to complement these systems and make them even more useful, such as wall-hung grids and racks to hold all manner of things from shoes to ties. These, of course, are more expensive than home-built solutions.

You should be aware that hangers have changed. There are now specialized hangers for specific garments, or multiples of garments (such as racks that hold up to half a dozen pairs of slacks on one hanger). These look better and may well treat your clothes better than the single-wire type.

Hanging garment bags have also found a place in the efficient closet. The large, clear, ventilated bags can be an extremely neat and safe way to store clothes not required every day. These, of course, can be used in any closet in the house.

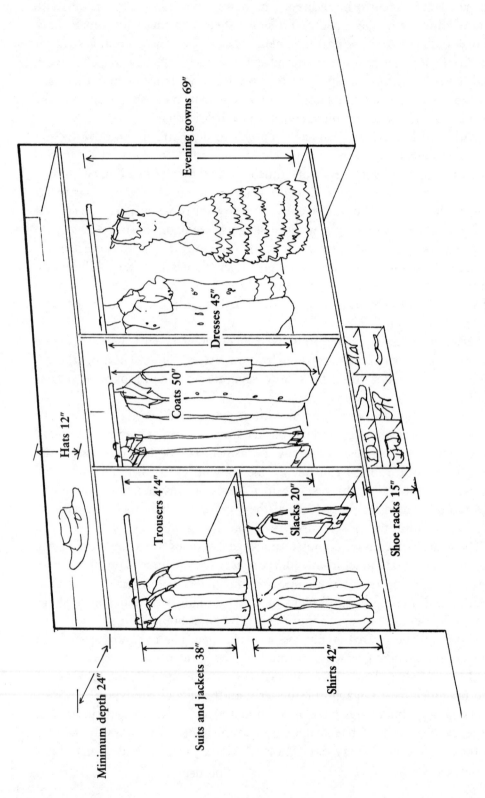

Figure 3.4 Typical dimensions for closet space

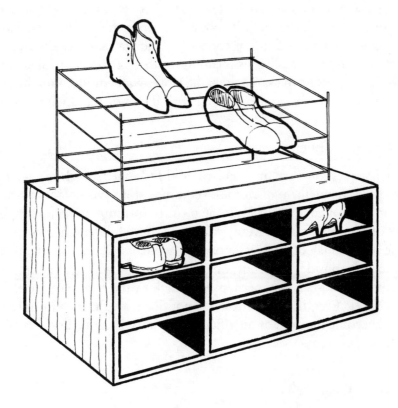

Figure 3.5   Racks and bins for shoes

Concealing—or Revealing—the Closet

The way in which the closet opens can also play a part in the use of the available space. Sliding doors, despite their contemporary look, are the least desirable. Not only are they prone to malfunction, but they make it impossible to see the entire closet at a glance. Nor can you use their back surfaces for tie racks and the like, since they must remain clear to slide past one another.

Folding doors, especially if ventilated, are more efficient. Much of the closet can be thrown open to view. But standard hinged doors are excellent for closets because you can see fully 90 percent of the closet when they're open, and they also allow all manner of small racks or shelves to be attached to their backs.

Covering the closet doors with mirrors does not actually create any extra space, but it does create the *illusion* of extra space. A small bedroom with an entire wall mirrored can seem twice as large—and a mirror, of course, is essential for careful dressing anyway.

At the same time, there is no absolute rule demanding doors at all. By dispensing with doors, it may be possible to use more space—perhaps in a corner or alcove—than would be possible if doors had to be installed. This storage plan comes close to the concept of the wall unit. If situated facing the bed, it becomes the obvious location for items that can or must be seen, such as the TV set. At the same time, the closet/wall unit need not be entirely open to view; sections can be covered with doors or fitted with drawers.

What About the Armoire?

There's no question that by itself, the old-fashioned wardrobe would not hold today's complement of clothes, yet it may still have a place in a modern bedroom. It is often a very handsome piece of furniture in its own right and can prove extremely useful. Many wardrobes have full-length mirrors; inside may be all manner of shelves and compartments. Rather than discarding such a piece, consider incorporating it into a new wall system of shelving and additional closet space, perhaps even making it the centerpiece of a wall-to-wall closet. Even if the wardrobe is not fine enough to be in full view, it may still become the core of an efficient closet, with all its drawers, shelves, and racks.

Other in-the-Room Units

Even if a closet is well fitted out, it may still be desirable to include more traditional pieces of clothes-storing furniture in the bedroom.

There are highboys, lowboys, and chests of drawers, along with other freestanding cabinets. Do not overlook the utility of the device known as a "gentleman's valet," which solves the problem of where to leave your clothes before retiring. It can be quite sophisticated, with accommodations for jackets, pants, or dresses. For this same purpose, you can use a tree-type coatrack in the corner of the room; many things can be hung on it and retrieved easily.

For items that are only occasionally used—clothes for skiing or swimming, for example—consider storage in places that, while not as easily reached as the main closet, make use of the less accessible areas of the room, such as high cabinets or shelves over alcoves or windows.

OTHER ITEMS

Sleeping and dressing may represent the main activities in a bedroom but do not necessarily cover every need. Dressing tables, well lit and provided with adequate mirrors and space for cosmetics, must also be considered, as well as some place or places for all the casual accessories that find their way into the bedroom. A simple nightstand may not be sufficient for the clock radio, telephone, glass of water, medicines, books and magazines, ashtrays, and lamps that gravitate to it, to say nothing of the nightly deposit of the contents of your pockets.

Also, as mentioned earlier, bedrooms sometimes double as guest rooms. When they are used for this purpose it is often nice to provide a few extra amenities, such as a place to sit and write a note or to eat.

Wall-hung shelving, freestanding chests, or even a table—of regular or coffee-table height—with an accompanying chair can simplify the problem of where to place all the occasional accessories we seem to accumulate. It may even give you somewhere to put a vase of flowers.

CHILDREN'S BEDROOMS

Much of what has been said about bedrooms in general applies especially to children's rooms. A child's room is usually used for many more activities than a simple bedroom; it's a private sanctum, play room, and study, as well as a place to sleep. As a result, whatever is provided in the way of storage must be integrated creatively with more functions than just storage and should be especially easy to use.

Easy-to-reach open bins and plenty of open shelving are the best ways to encourage at least a modicum of tidiness. Bear in mind that children sometimes grow faster than your plans can be realized. It is best to arrange something quickly, even if it is simple, and then adapt it for another use in a short while—for example, a platform area for a bassinet can later be converted to a child's play desk.

4

THE BATHROOM

There was a time when the bathroom was a far more insignificant place than it is today. Before the era of running water, much personal washing was commonly done in the bedroom with a jug and basin on a sideboard, and the toilet was often not in the house at all, existing only as a separate "privy" or "outhouse."

There is still debate over whether the toilet should be included in the bathroom or be located separately. The confusion that exists with the names we use for these places is one indication of this: bathroom, toilet, lavatory, rest room, and washroom. Nevertheless, the majority of new houses are constructed with "bathrooms" that contain a shower and/or a tub, a sink or lavatory counter, *and* a toilet.

The metamorphosis of the "bathroom" does not stop there, however. In many American motel and hotel rooms, for example, the demarcation between bedroom and bathroom is not always distinct; there is frequently a kind of transitional space given over to a dressing area, often with a sink separate from the enclosed shower and toilet. In private homes bathrooms are also becoming more versatile. The master bathroom in particular is often much less of a separate room than it used to be. Furthermore, the inclusion of extra facilities such as bidets, saunas, and whirlpools has become increasingly common.

Even in houses less opulently appointed, the bathroom often serves as a place to apply cosmetics, monitor health, and perform first aid—especially in households with small children and the inevitable succession of bumps and scrapes.

All in all, the bathroom is now one of the more important rooms in a house, one in which a good deal of time is spent and to which considerably more attention is paid than used to be the case. As a result, besides the sink, toilet, and tub, we now need to provide for a wide range of supplies and equipment—products for our teeth and hair, medicines, first aid supplies, cosmetics, soaps and shampoos, towels, laundry, children's bath toys, and such extras as scales, steps, and seating for whirlpools or steam rooms. The bathroom may not be as small as it once was, but often it is still too small for everything we'd like it to contain. Nevertheless, there is often undeveloped space in the room, if we know where to look and how to use it.

BATHING

Bathing is one of the primary uses of the bathroom; it involves certain equipment and supplies that we must accommodate.

The very smallest bathroom may have only a shower stall and a sink. Yet even here, certain items are just as indispensable as in a more luxuriously fitted room. Among the things needed by almost everyone are soap, shampoo, washcloths, back scrubbers and other assorted brushes and sponges, as well as shower caps.

Simply leaving these items on the floor of the shower or the edge of the tub is inconvenient and potentially dangerous. At the very least, a soap dish should be provided, preferably a self-draining one. If your bathroom has no built-in soap dish, there are numerous designs that can be glued or screwed to the wall. Others hang from the shower head, or are supported in a basket hung on the side of the tub or on a tray across the tub, from side to side.

Plastic-coated wire mini-baskets or shelving make ideal storage space for items that are often wet. Such units may be horizontal or vertical. One variety is designed to fit a corner space so that a small shower stall does not become even more cramped (see figure 4.1). Molded plastic racks that can be suspended from faucets or shower heads also make ideal places to keep soap and bottles of shampoo and hair conditioner. They are sometimes provided with hooks or bars from which washcloths and other items, such as shower caps, may be hung.

Many newer shower stalls are now made as complete units out of molded plastic and incorporate shelf space, storage niches, and soap ledges so that places are already provided for whatever is needed while showering. Bathtubs, however, remain relatively hostile to the things we take with us when

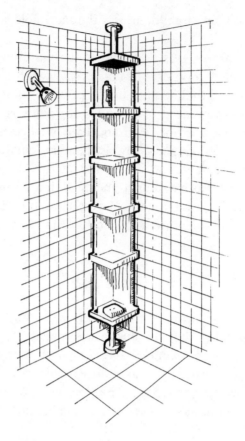

Figure 4.1   Bathroom corner unit

we step into a hot bath; unless there are fixtures already built into the wall near at hand, it can be difficult to know even where to put the soap. This shortcoming is all the more complicated when small children are involved, since it is often difficult to get them into the tub in the first place without a bevy of rubber ducks, boats, and other toys.

There are several solutions to the tub problem. Already mentioned is the wide, plastic- or vinyl-coated wire rack that reaches from one side of the tub to the other. However, these often get in the way when bathing, and the poorly designed ones have an annoying habit of falling into the tub. There are also floating racks made of lightweight plastic, which can be kept in the water; these may be the most convenient. Also, some form of shelving can be provided adjacent to the tub. This need not be attached to the wall, although that is often the simplest solution. The shelving can take the form of a cabinet the same height as the tub. Now you have a place to put things, as well as a place to sit if you're bathing a child. In really cramped bathrooms, such a bathside cabinet can be fitted with wheels or casters allowing it to be moved out of the way when it's not being used (see figure 4.2). Old-

Figure 4.2   Movable bathside cabinet

fashioned, freestanding tubs are ideal for a tub-surround modernization; they can be boxed in in such a way that a lot of usable surface space is provided at the ends or sides of the tub.

Although showers are so popular that most tubs are fitted out to serve as shower stalls, there are still those who are satisfied with just a tub for bathing. If no provision for showering is needed, you can use space above the tub as a place for shelves or cabinets. Just be sure that objects stored there cannot fall into the tub.

CLOTHING

The bathroom is not the ideal place to store clothing because of the humidity created there, even if you have an exhaust fan and adequate ventilation. Nevertheless, some provision should be made for clothing taken off during bathing or showering. It should not simply be dumped on the floor.

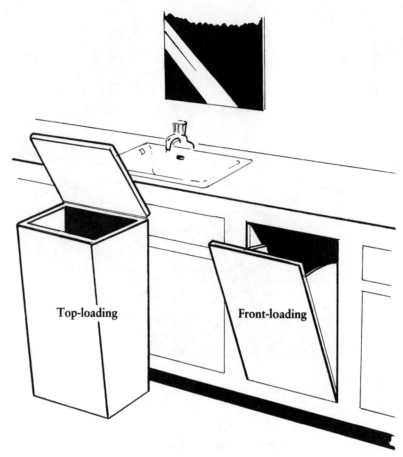

Figure 4.3   Laundry hampers

A hook behind the door is minimal. Why not provide a three-way hook, or even tiered hooks, so that several pieces of clothing can be hung and reclaimed without having to remove the whole collection each time? There may even be space between the head of the tub and the wall to construct a narrow closet that, with the help of the closet organizers described in the previous chapter, can hold several bathrobes, as well as hooks for other incidental clothing.

Of course, not all clothing needs to be hung; some may be ready for the laundry. The bathroom is certainly a logical place for the laundry hamper, especially if the washing machine is located there. (Some bathrooms even have an access chute to the laundry room on a lower level.) If the hamper is freestanding, instead of being built into the wall or under a counter, the top can be used as a temporary resting place for shed clothes. Use of the top for any purpose is much easier if the hamper is a front-loading rather than a top-loading type (see figure 4.3).

A tree-type coatrack can provide additional clothing storage. This can be especially convenient in bathrooms where it is not possible to use the behind-door area, since these coatracks are easily moved into the smallest space.

Care of clothing in the bathroom also involves drying racks, for laundry items that should be drip-dried. The area over the tub is the ideal site for these. A shower curtain rod, however, is not really suitable; it allows the items to drip half in the tub and half on the floor. Instead, install a retractable drying line fixture; it mounts on the wall at either end of the tub (or shower). Or, from two hooks in the ceiling above the tub, you can suspend a rod centered over the tub. Less convenient—since it has to be removed every time you desire to use the tub—but often capable of holding more, is a collapsible wooden clothes rack that stands in the tub.

BATH AND HAND TOWELS

In almost any bathroom, you can find nooks and crannies—at the head of tubs, behind shower walls, over windows, or behind doors—that could lend themselves to the construction of small cabinets or closets, certainly some additional open shelves at the least, to store clean towels and supplies of toilet paper and facial tissues. Project 9 (page 136) shows a small over-door cabinet.

Towels in use should have their own racks—not towel rings, which do not allow towels to dry well—and there should be at least as many racks in a bathroom as there are regular users of the bathroom. No matter how the bathroom walls are finished, there's always a way to attach such racks. A hardware store should have all the available options for firmly attaching racks to any kind of wall. When installing new towel racks, consider the advantages of one long rack, perhaps extending the length of a wall or a countertop, rather than several individual ones (see figure 4.4). You can usually gain space for two or more towels, and the bar allows towels to dry efficiently. If this is impossible, and wall space is really at a minimum, towel racks mounted one above the other, while not perfect (the towels will usually overlap), are better than only one. You really need racks; towels will not dry if draped over the edge of the tub or chairs.

If you're addicted to a warm towel, install an electrically heated towel rack. Draping a towel over a radiator will limit the radiator's efficiency more than it will increase your comfort with a warm towel. Another solution, which uses the heat from the radiator without inhibiting its efficiency, is to mount a towel rack *above* the radiator.

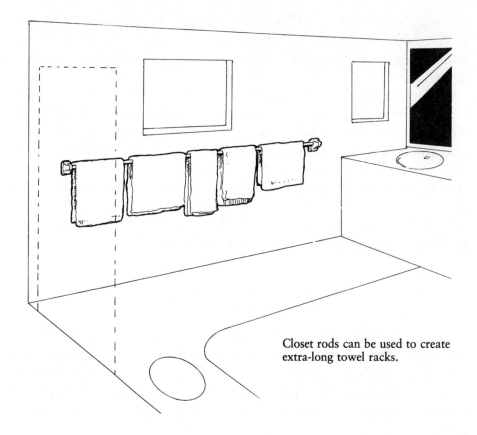

Closet rods can be used to create
extra-long towel racks.

Figure 4.4   Long towel rack

THE MEDICINE CABINET

An almost universal fixture in every bathroom, no matter how small or otherwise poorly equipped, is the wall-mounted, so-called medicine cabinet. Typically it is positioned over the sink and fitted with a mirrored door.

While a genuine cabinet for medicines would undoubtedly be a great advantage in a bathroom, it would have to be both large enough for the medicines it is expected to contain and secure enough from inadvertent inspection by inquisitive children. With these requirements, the typical over-the-sink unit is invariably too small and too easily opened. Assuming that you remove potentially dangerous drugs and medicines from this cabinet, consider what really needs to be kept here. The list can be astonishingly long: soaps, toothpaste, shampoo, conditioners, hair spray, razors, razor blades, scissors, combs, brushes, hair pins, tweezers, dental floss, nail files, cologne, after-shave, talcum powder, deodorant, mouthwash, hand cream, and on and on. It should be obvious that for most of us the typical medicine cabinet is pathetically inadequate. What to do? First, find separate storage for some of these items, then consider how a larger cabinet can replace the small one.

In fact, rather than simply replacing your cabinet with a larger one, you could gain much more space by constructing a wall unit across the entire wall above the sink. The shelving, which can be fitted with doors or not as design dictates, can be compartmentalized to provide much more logical storage than is possible within the cramped confines of a tiny medicine cabinet. The section immediately above the sink should, of course, be mirrored, and if the bathroom is small, the use of additional mirrors can lessen the feeling of confinement. As an alternative, mirrored doors can effectively conceal the clutter contained by all this extra shelf space.

CABINET AND COUNTERTOP UNITS

Two other areas that offer possibilities for storing quantities of bathroom accessories are the spaces under and adjacent to the sink. Although there are extremely beautiful modern freestanding sink units available, it often makes sense to replace these and old-fashioned pedestal sinks with countertop drop-ins; an entire cabinet can be created under the sink this way. Such a cabinet is an ideal location for the bathroom cleaning equipment, such as toilet-bowl brushes, cleaning powders, and sponges and brushes. Even the wastebasket, a necessary item in the well-equipped bathroom, can be kept inside this cabinet, especially if the under-sink plumbing seriously restricts the shelf space potential. If such a cabinet containing a sink is also constructed as a wall unit and reaches from one wall to another, not only will useful extra counter space be created but more storage space will be provided for various small appliances such as electric toothbrushes, shavers, hair driers, and electric massagers. (See chapter 5, "The Kitchen," for a full discussion of how such cabinet space can be best utilized.)

Should there be absolutely no room for conventional rectangular shelving or cabinetry, consider the possibility of getting more out of your corners by installing triangular shelves (see figure 4.5).

DISPLAY STORAGE

If it is not practical to incorporate the sink into a countertop, it is usually still possible to build at least a simple bookcase-style shelving unit somewhere in the bathroom. This can hold at least some towels and supplies. Open shelves can also be very attractive, turning storage into display. This works especially well with colorful items such as soaps, which can be kept in

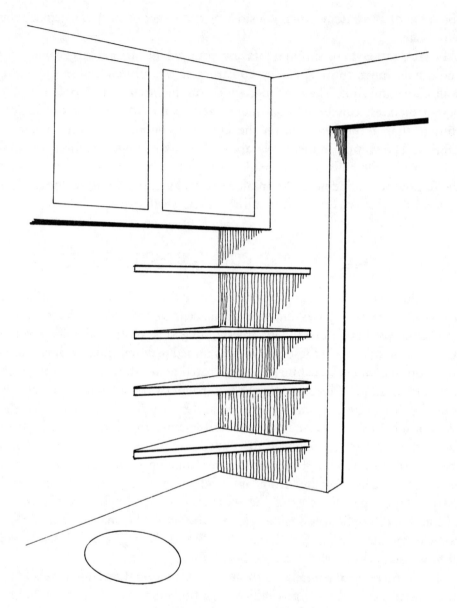

Figure 4.5 Triangular shelves

attractive baskets, and pretty towels. Open racks or hanging containers can hold a great deal, look attractive, and be very convenient in a bathroom otherwise short on cabinet or shelving space. That may free up enclosed closet space for less attractive items.

There are some items that are just too large and obtrusive to be conveniently stored away, even if a place could be found for them. Some, such as scales, are best simply accepted as part of the bathroom furniture. Plants, both on the floor and hanging, can sometimes be successfully deployed to disguise or camouflage such awkward items.

WALL FIXTURES

There is one more class of storage that is peculiarly applicable to the bathroom: the wall-mounted fixture. Properly speaking, this includes towel racks of all kinds, already discussed. But many more pieces of bathroom equipment may be gotten out of the way by being fixed to the wall at appropriate spots. Small appliances such as electric shavers and toothbrushes are obvious examples, but there are also tissue dispensers, toothbrush racks, and racks for hairbrushes. Even small fold-down bathroom scales can be wall mounted just at the floor line.

Equally adaptable to the same kind of wall-hung storage are the backs of any doors in the bathroom—the entry door, any closet or cabinet door, and perhaps even the outside of the shower door. Shallow shelves or racks can fit much of the door area, providing locations for all manner of small items.

OTHER AMENITIES

For many people the bathroom can be a temporary refuge from a crowded and perpetually busy life, and, as such, a book or magazine rack is not out of place there. A small open magazine rack located on the wall convenient to the toilet, or even built around it, can be useful and attractive. However, if you decide on a book rack or small shelf unit built above the toilet, be sure to leave sufficient space (at least 12 inches) over the tank so that it may be opened easily if necessary for servicing or repair. Project 10 shows a simple reading rack (see page 140).

If the room is large enough to be made more luxurious, consider comfortable seating—an armchair, perhaps, in which to relax after a session in the steam room or a soaking in the tub. This would make the provision of a small bookcase and side table even more appropriate.

5

THE KITCHEN

Today's kitchen, like the contemporary living room, has become a combination of previously separate areas and has to serve not only as a kitchen—a place to cook food—but also as a pantry and informal eating area where food and supplies are stored, prepared, and served. Although there is now something of a trend back toward "country kitchens" large enough to serve as informal family gathering and eating places, for a long time kitchens have been shrinking in size.

Offsetting this loss of space has been the increase in efficient labor-saving devices that have considerably reduced the onus of many kitchen chores. Gone is the old-fashioned kitchen stove; in its place are compact, efficient gas or electric cooking centers, and often the speedy microwave oven.

Nevertheless, although dominated by major appliances, the kitchen is still expected to be home to more objects than any other room in the house. Practically all of these objects are required to be easily accessible every time the kitchen is used. For this to happen with any degree of convenience, you must concentrate on understanding what goes on in the kitchen and arranging things accordingly.

The ideal kitchen should be laid out in such a way that the main operations—food storage, preparation, cooking, serving, and cleaning up—can be carried out in the most efficient manner possible. Once this is done, the storage of utensils and equipment will fall into place far more easily. It will not be a matter of cramming food and dishes higgledy-piggledy wherever possible.

The basic idea is to maintain a "working triangle" between the sink, the range, and the refrigerator with sufficient counter space in between so that work can progress in a continuous flow from one area to the other. There should be minimum backtracking necessary and, if possible, no interruptions from traffic routes passing through the kitchen.

There are tried and tested floor plans that will achieve an efficient work flow. Four simple ones are shown in Figure 5.1: an in-line layout, where everything is arranged along one wall; a parallel galley-style layout, where two cabinet runs face each other; and **U**-shaped and **L**-shaped layouts, so arranged that the working triangle can be followed sequentially from one area to another.

Unfortunately, we don't always have control over how our kitchens are laid out and are forced to compromise. But with the "ideal" pattern in mind, we can very often make small adjustments that add up to a major improvement. One way of doing this, for example, is to incorporate a work island into the plan; it can often provide the missing link in an efficient chain of

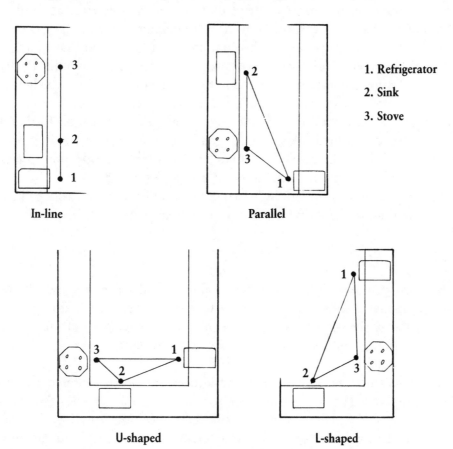

1. Refrigerator

2. Sink

3. Stove

In-line

Parallel

U-shaped

L-shaped

Figure 5.1 Working triangles

operations. It might even be possible to create a mobile island to further ease the constraints of a poorly designed kitchen.

Once you have organized the kitchen into storage, cleaning, cooking, and preparation areas (in your mind, at least, if not in every physical detail), more items not only will find a home but also will become more accessible at the point of use, increasing the kitchen's efficiency and making life a lot easier and more pleasant.

FOOD STORAGE

There are several classes of food that are kept in the typical kitchen: perishable, nonperishable, dry, and canned. Some of these are commonly bought in small amounts as required on a day-to-day (or at most, a week-to-week) basis, while others are bought in bulk as convenient and kept until needed. Once you recognize this and don't try to keep everything right in the kitchen, you can often free up space for items that must always be close at hand.

Although it is certainly more convenient to unload and store the groceries in one place, sometimes there is just not enough room to do that in a tiny kitchen. Consider keeping at least those extra, emergency supplies of dry foods and canned goods in a spare closet or cabinet elsewhere in the house, re-creating, in a sense, the old-fashioned larder.

Similarly, a basement, if available, is certainly a good location for items needing cool, dark areas. An area designated a wine cellar, no matter how modest, can also store other foodstuffs such as canned goods, put-up preserves, or relatively nonperishable items like apples and potatoes.

For items that must be stored frozen, a separate freezer can easily be kept elsewhere than in the kitchen, since access is required only infrequently.

Inside the Kitchen

Regardless of how much food you are able to find places for *outside* the kitchen, it makes most sense to try to arrange whatever food storage you keep *in* the kitchen in the same area, simply for convenience of unbagging when returning from the store and ready access when cooking.

The refrigerator. Food storage in the kitchen should be centered around the refrigerator. The modern refrigerator is a mixed blessing. Although it has eliminated the need for daily shopping, it does take up a lot of space. However, if properly integrated into a surround of counters and cabinets, it does not have to dominate the kitchen.

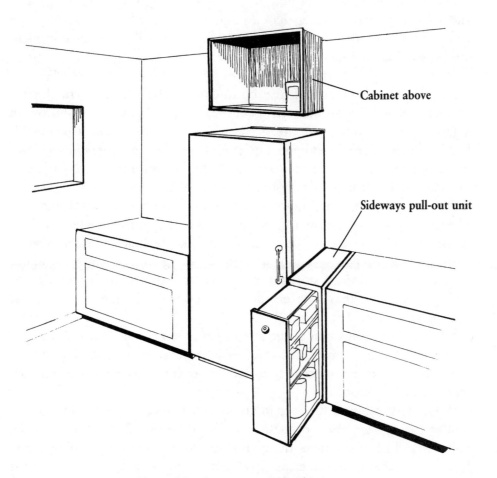

Cabinet above

Sideways pull-out unit

Figure 5.2   Storage around refrigerator

Many refrigerators, not including the so-called "side-by-sides," are so designed that you can rehang the door from the opposite side. That can sometimes dramatically improve the refrigerator's compatibility within the working triangle. This points up the fact that a food storage area also needs to be adjacent to counter space; any system of cabinetry into which the refrigerator fits should also contain provision for this.

Many refrigerators are so tall that the shallow space above them is often wasted. Yet this area can provide a perfect spot for infrequently needed items, such as canned supplies and bulk storage, from which weekly or monthly amounts may be drawn as needed. Similarly, make use of the odd spaces often left at one side or the other of a refrigerator, if it is not built into its own niche. Even the width of a foot or less is enough to be used as a pull-out shelf unit (see figure 5.2), or a slotted unit for trays.

In the same way that space may be gained by having a separate refrigerator and a separate freezer rather than a single refrigerator/freezer, it may make sense to have a second refrigerator, especially a smaller, more convenient model, such as an under-the-counter type.

Cabinets. The hallmark of the up-to-date kitchen is its ultra-efficient cabinetry. Regardless of the style, be it New England paneling or European high-tech, how cabinets are arranged on the inside can make a major difference in their usable storage capacity. There are innumerable ways to improve on the basic cabinet—one simply fitted with one or two shelves—including pull-out units, swing-out units, revolving units, unfolding racks, sliding compartments, and units fitted to the backs of the doors themselves. The key to planning the interior cabinet fittings is to make whatever is kept in the cabinet easily accessible at all times. This precludes filling up shelves with cans and packets several rows deep. If a large number of small items, such as cans, need to be stored in a cabinet, at least provide a revolving or pull-out system so that a dozen cans do not have to be removed to get at the one you want.

An equally obvious point, but one which is sometimes overlooked, is to store the everyday items in the most easily reached places, putting once-a-week or once-a-month items in floor-level spaces or areas that can be reached only with a step stool.

If you have cabinets that are in an interior corner, there are various solutions for making their deepest recesses accessible. But along with the pullouts and revolving units there may be another solution: gaining access from the other side. In some cases, you can open up the back of the cabinet from an adjacent room, either creating separate storage for that room or using the space from both sides. This is often a useful way of making dishes available to both the kitchen and the dining room.

Last, when organizing your cabinet space around the refrigerator, plan to include a drawer or shelf for the freezer containers, plastic bags, wrap, and foil that are used in the storing of foodstuffs. Also useful is a shelf or rack to hold used grocery bags, since these should be recycled as garbage containers or can liners. Project 11 shows a simple bag holder (see page 143).

Open display. Many food items need not be hidden away; on the contrary, they can enhance the atmosphere of a working kitchen: strings of sausages, garlic chains, and dried herbs are just a few. Hung from hooks or in open baskets, they can add to the charm as well as the efficiency of a kitchen. Bowls of fruit also lend color and provide opportunities for healthy snacking.

THE KITCHEN SINK

The kitchen sink forms the center of the next most important part of the working triangle. A lot goes on here, from rinsing, washing, and trimming of food to the cleanup necessary during and after cooking. All too often the area around the sink can become an untidy jumble of drying racks, pot scourers, cutting boards, cleaning powders, table and cookware—both dirty and clean. This area usually includes (if you're lucky enough to have them) the dishwasher, the garbage compactor, and the garbage disposal. Once again, a little forethought about the way these are organized can result in less clutter and greater efficiency, and perhaps more space where little or none was apparent before.

Sink Accessories

Ideally there should be at least three feet of counter space on either side of the sink, whether it is a double or a single unit. Furthermore, as much of this area as possible should be kept clear, so it can easily be used for its primary functions, preparing food and cleaning up. To this end, keep as many of the sink-side tools as possible on hooks, racks, or on handy shelves.

A plastic or wood stacking rack can be a great space-saver for soaps, steel wool pads, bottle brushes, and the like. There is often space for these things on a narrow shelf fixed immediately above the sink, especially if the sink is located under a window, as many are.

The cabinet below the sink is also ideal for odd items such as dish-towel racks, dish drainers, scrubbers and scourers, buckets and scrub brushes, and wastebaskets. These should all have individual homes, if possible, not simply be allowed to accumulate on the floor. Some custom arrangements should be made, since this under-sink area usually houses plumbing that would interfere with normal shelving. Without restricting access to this plumbing, arrange hooks, racks, and slide-out accessories to hold as many of your cleaning and sink tools as possible.

Paper-towel holders can usually find a convenient home on the wall by the sink, on the side of an adjacent cabinet, or even under an upper cabinet.

There is often a certain amount of space, invariably overlooked, inside the sink cabinet and immediately in front of the sink. This is usually too shallow for a conventional drawer (because the sink itself is in the way), but it can be turned into a shallow cubby accessed by a tilt-down door (see figure 5.3). This can be the ideal spot for sponges, brushes, and soap pads.

A backing to this shelf is essential to keep items from falling into the cabinet space below.

Back panel

Figure 5.3   Tilt-down sink shelf and door

GARBAGE

Arrangements for garbage disposal take many forms: freestanding containers with foot-pedal-operated lids, trash compactors, and sink-mounted disposal units. This last kind, while convenient, is not sound ecologically since it can use excessive amounts of water for the amount of garbage disposed. A better idea is to provide several containers—freestanding, or located in pull-out, slide-out, or tip-out drawers—into which garbage, disposable and recyclable material can be emptied separately. The area immediately beneath the sink is ideal for garbage, since you can dump in waste from food being washed and trimmed, as well as scraps that are cleaned off dishes before they are washed or loaded into the dishwasher.

One item, useful in itself but also of help in waste disposal, is a pull-out cutting board. Located directly below the counter surface, adjacent to the sink, it makes disposal of food-preparation waste directly into under-sink garbage containers both easy and clean.

As more and more people recycle, either from personal choice or because their community requires it, more and more planning centers around trash disposal. Although contemporary kitchens are now designed with recycling bins, a separate trash container for every category of trash—paper, metal, clear glass, colored glass, and so forth—is generally impractical in many kitchens. To save on space, consider having two bins in addition to garbage, one for disposable and one for recyclable trash. The recyclable container can then be taken to larger cans in another area of the house, such as the basement, garage, or even outside, for sorting.

TABLEWARE

Dishes may be left to dry in racks at the side of the sink or put directly into the dishwasher, but eventually they will need to be put away. If their permanent home is nearby, in a cabinet near the sink, they will be put away more often. A compromise is to use open wood racks above the sink counter space or even directly above the sink itself so that when wet, dishes may be allowed to drip right into the sink.

Similarly, cups and saucers, mugs, glasses, bowls, and cutlery all need a place to be stored before and after washing. Organizing your cabinets around the sink to contain these items will make their storage easy—and discourage their accumulation in and around the sink itself.

Anything with a handle—not just cups—can be hung from cup hooks; this can often free up severely limited shelf space. Such hanging items can be arranged not only under the shelves in a cabinet but also along the front edge of open shelving or even around a window frame and from wall-mounted racks. Mug trees, kept on countertops also used for snacking, further free precious cabinet space while keeping the mugs handy and tidy.

Stemware is another class of tableware that can be stored in a hanging position; glass racks can often make use of overhead space unsuited for anything else (see page 20).

One of the greatest improvements you can make is to separate out in compartmentalized storage the numerous classes of cutlery. All too often, it finds its way into one jumbled mess in a single drawer. The best set of flatware is often kept in the dining room or in a china-cabinet drawer (see page 19), but every kitchen accumulates extra knives, forks, spoons, ladles, and stirrers, as well as many other awkward-to-store implements such as strainers, serving spoons, whisks, and spatulas. There are also a lot of other small items such as cheese slicers, egg slicers, can openers, corkscrews, and potato peelers that can find their way into this chaos. Use compartmentalized containers that fit into drawers or stand alone on shelves to separate these items. Hang as many as possible on racks near the stove where they will be used, and keep odd items in jars or upright containers. The key here is to divide and conquer the clutter.

COOKING

The third main element of the working triangle and the very heart of the kitchen is the range. Formerly one unit, and often a large unit at that, this may now be in separate parts, such as a countertop burner, a wall-mounted oven and broiler unit, and increasingly common, a microwave oven. The microwave can sometimes be mounted in the wall.

Splitting up the cooking function this way may help a small kitchen organize its cooking facilities more efficiently, but for serious cooks, a full-fledged restaurant-style stove is still considered the ne plus ultra of facilities. In either case, however, just as with the sink center, the ideal arrangement is one that includes a certain amount of countertop adjacent to the cooking unit or units. It does no good to save floor space by having a wall-mounted oven and then having to walk across the kitchen each time to put down whatever you take out of the oven.

Pots and Pans

The counter next to the range (or wall oven) should be heatproof, of course, but equally important is that it should be kept clear of unused pots and pans. These are most efficiently hung above or near the stove from straight or circular racks so that they are always within reach. Their visibility gives the kitchen an air of no-nonsense practicality. Many people prefer things put away, feeling more comfortable with a cleaner look, but if that means cramming all your pots and pans into difficult-to-reach base cabinets, it's not really practical. That's especially true if, in order to save space, small saucepans are nested inside larger ones. If pots and pans must be put away, provide each with its own, *easily accessible* space. Getting down on your hands and knees to find a missing lid for a particular pot among a jumble of pots and pans is an example of a storage system almost worse than useless. Don't even consider using the oven or broiler as a storage space; you'll be forever loading and unloading it.

The best way to store a lot of pots and pans in a deep cabinet is to make use of sliding shelves or pull-out units. Each item can have its own space and can be removed or replaced without interfering with any of the others. If the cabinet chosen to store these items is located in a corner, install a lazy Susan inside so that the full depth can be used without having to grope into the farthest reaches. Don't restrict your thinking about a lazy Susan to one cabinet. Open, floor-to-ceiling revolving-shelf units can also be installed, making hitherto unused corners useful again.

Traditional cooking stoves, unless installed at the same time the cabinetry in the kitchen was designed, tend to create odd spaces at either side. Since it is not always advisable to locate stoves right next to a side wall, a small space is often left, too narrow for a standard cabinet and counter (but large enough to accumulate dustpans, small brooms, and the like). Get rid of this hard-to-clean gap by installing a narrow pull-out unit designed to hold a single depth of pots and pans. Project 12 shows a typical pull-out unit (see page 145).

Utensils

Almost as vital as pots and pans are the utensils needed when cooking. Things like spatulas, strainers, mashers, sieves, stirrers, spoons, and ladles should all be within easy reach. Perhaps most important of all, this list should include pot holders, which must be on hand the *moment* they are needed. This does not mean crammed into a drawer on the other side of the kitchen. Most of these items can be hung from a series of hooks, through holes in their handles, or kept in racks (magnetically or in properly sized slots). They will then be more convenient when needed, and that untidy drawer will be kept free for other storage.

Where to hang such utensils, and pots too, depends on the particular arrangement of the cooking facilities. Directly over the stove is fine so long as sufficient clearance is allowed for safety's sake. Ideally there should be a hood over gas or electric burners, or at least some kind of exhaust fan, to keep the kitchen free of excess steam and cooking odors.

If you have an exhaust hood, the space over it is usually too high for easy access. This is the ideal location for those odd accessories not needed every day, such as roasting racks and baking pans. Similarly, in kitchens equipped with ovens and broilers built into cabinets, the topmost and bottommost cabinets should be used for seldom-required objects.

Herbs and Condiments

One of the best arrangements for a cooktop is to have it accessible from all sides. This avoids any reaching over flames or steaming pots. Island cooktops provide this kind of convenience and at the same time offer many other advantages. For one thing, you can install shallow recessed shelving on all sides, which is singularly well suited for small containers of condiments, herbs, and spices used while cooking.

Even if you don't have an island, it's not hard to find space for a spice

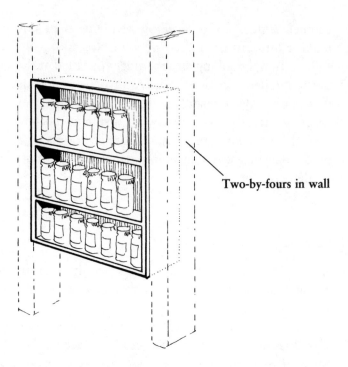

Two-by-fours in wall

Figure 5.4   Recessed spice shelves

rack. It can be mounted on the wall, on the side of a cabinet, or even on the inside of a cabinet door. It should not take up counter space. It may even be possible to make a recessed spice shelf by opening up part of an interior wall in the same way that many bathroom medicine cabinets are installed (see figure 5.4).

FOOD PREPARATION

Throughout this chapter we have stressed the importance of adequate counter space around each of the working areas. Ideally there should be a fourth area, consisting primarily of counter space dedicated to various aspects of what is best called "preparation." This is where food is processed with any of the innumerable appliances that crowd the modern kitchen—the place where it is weighed, floured, basted, wiped, and cut before being consigned to stove or broiler. This is also where it is finally transferred onto platters or into tureens prior to serving.

You may have so many mixing bowls and small appliances that there isn't room for them on the counter. Actually, the counter should be kept as clear as possible so you have room to work, as well as to keep it clean for proper food handling. To be used, however, all the bowls and appliances must be easily available. Consider shallow, open shelves built along a wall where there may not be enough space for a full-depth cabinet. Such an area is often discovered near a door or in a corner. Some items, like waffle irons, may be low enough to occupy small shelves attached under upper cabinets. Places may also be found for certain appliances on narrow open shelves attached to the side of a cabinet.

If you really need to increase your counter space for major operations, such as serving out portions on many plates, add lids to the top drawers (under the countertop). When these drawers are pulled out extra surface is provided.

The preparation zone is also the ideal location for cookbooks, loose recipes, and shopping lists. As a last thought, this part of the kitchen might also serve, when cooking is not actually in progress, as a substitute office space, particularly if there's a place for a small typewriter and somewhere to keep household bills and accounts.

6

LAUNDRY/UTILITY ROOMS

Older and larger houses often have separate laundry rooms or other odd rooms and adjuncts off the main kitchen area, but smaller and more recent houses are less likely to be so generously equipped. Yet every home has need for such a space. Practically everyone needs to take care of laundry, even if only to store it, and we all need a place in which to do the jobs and store the tools and supplies necessary to maintain a home. Old paperwork, cleaning supplies, all the odds and ends of hardware worth keeping, such as extra tiles, carpet pieces, light bulbs, and even pet paraphernalia, are just a few of the things that call for a "utility room."

Even if you have no separate laundry/utility room, it would be a good idea to set aside some place to fulfill that need. There are many candidates— a back entrance, a passage or corridor, a small area off to one side of the kitchen, a former pantry, or a space that can be claimed in the basement, garage, or closed porch. Wherever you can find the space, a laundry/utility room will prove to be of great value. In this chapter, we'll cover what you may want to keep and use in such a space, whether it's an actual room or just an area set aside, and how best to optimize what may be a less-than-perfect location.

THE SECOND ENTRANCE

There is usually only one entrance into an apartment, but practically all detached or semidetached houses have both a front door and a back door. This side or rear entrance is invaluable as a potential safety exit in case of fire or other emergency. It is the ideal location for a fire extinguisher. While it's important to keep a fire extinguisher close to any potential source of fire, such as in the kitchen, having one just inside an entrance can be very useful since everyone will know where it is and it will be easily accessible in an emergency. The second entrance is often adjacent to the kitchen, giving it that advantage as well.

Delivery Entrance

In many situations, especially in older houses in rural or semirural areas, the front door may now be used less than the back door. In some cases, there is no longer adequate parking in front of the main entrance; in others, it may just have become more convenient to bring the groceries in through the back door. In any event, the back door is often better suited to deliveries. Being less formally decorated, there is less to worry about when carrying in large and possibly dirty packages and objects. If there is room, the area just inside the back door can provide a perfect location for washing machines or for storage of rougher household necessities. If this is an entrance that you use when you're wet or dirty, it would be very useful to find space there to hold and to hang wet raincoats.

Pets

The back entrance is often the best place to store pet paraphernalia as well: litter trays and supplies, brushes, collars and leashes, flea collars and medications, as well as carrying boxes and bulky food supplies. Of course, feeding your pets in this area may also be preferable to the nuisance of having pet bowls underfoot in the kitchen.

THE HOME OFFICE

An antique desk, if you have one, can be an attractive addition to a living room, den, or library. That's one way to solve the home office problem. A separate room devoted to at-home work is a more elaborate solution. For many people, however, whose paperwork needs are not so great and whose space is limited, the utility room can be the perfect place to find room for

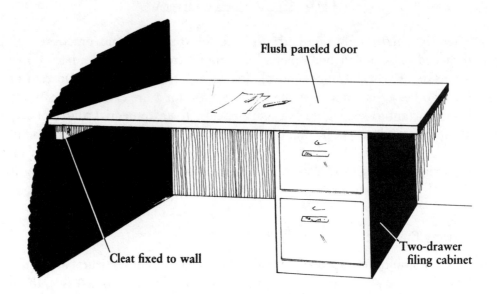

Figure 6.1   Home office

a desk. In any case, having a specific place to organize and pay the household bills makes for better accounting and better housekeeping.

A simple yet efficient mini-office can be created by supporting a board or flush-paneled door on a two-drawer filing cabinet at one end and a cleat fixed to the wall at the other end (see figure 6.1). This setup can provide all the space you need to write checks, make grocery lists, answer letters, and perform other office chores.

If you are equipped with a typewriter, word processor, or even a computer, more substantial provision will be required. Still, if you put your equipment on mobile stands or equip it with casters, enabling it to be rolled out of the way when not in use, the laundry/utility room can still serve as its space.

Every household has some precious, important, or irreplaceable items that, for whatever reason, are not suitable for a bank's safety deposit box. Still, they need protection against fire and theft. The utility room may be the ideal location to install an appropriately rated wall or floor safe. In such a room, you can more easily bolt things to the floor or cut holes in the wall.

THE LAUNDRY

Household laundry is obviously much easier to do now than it was before universal plumbing, and the equipment takes up less space. It's possible today to handle the laundry with a single washer-dryer unit rolled into a corner in practically any room in the house.

The vast majority of homes, however, have a separate washing machine and clothes dryer, usually found, if not in a separate laundry room, then close to the kitchen or perhaps in the basement. The ideal arrangement—a dedicated laundry room—will also contain a large laundry sink, laundry storage facilities, and space for folding and ironing.

Wherever the laundry is actually done, providing for its orderly accumulation can greatly improve the efficiency of the operation. One large basket or hamper into which everything is thrown is the simplest solution, but a sorting system of some kind works much better. It may be nothing more than a couple of bins fixed to the wall, adjacent to or in between the washing machine and the clothes dryer. When closed, the lids to these bins will form an ideal surface for sorting or folding, space for which is often hard to find.

If the laundry room (or area) is in the basement or even downstairs from bathrooms and bedrooms, you might install a chute. Bins at the bottom of the chute could not only receive laundry tossed down the chute but also provide work space for subsequent sorting.

If the laundry is done in an area adjacent to the bedroom or the bathroom it may even make sense to cut a hole in the common wall in much the same way as firewood is sometimes fed from the outside to a fireplace.

Large laundry sinks are useful for preliminary cleaning and soaking and, if they have a cover, can be used as folding or general work surfaces. A simple cover of wood or plywood is sufficient, although a plastic laminate countertop is easier to keep clean and may fit better into the rest of the decor. Such a sink can be boxed in, providing space underneath eminently suitable for laundry and cleaning supplies.

Clean Laundry

Once the laundry has been washed, it is either drip-dried or put into the clothes dryer. Some people still prefer to hang the laundry outside to dry, but not many situations make this possible anymore. For items that *must* be drip-dried inside, some sort of drying rack is a necessity. You can reduce the time needed for drying and free the area for other operations by directing a fan at the drying area. In cramped quarters, consider racks that can be hauled up to the ceiling on pulleys, out of the way, but positioned over a sink or a tub to catch the drips. Multi-armed racks that swing out from the wall are another alternative.

After drying comes folding and/or ironing. Various ways to provide work surfaces for folding have already been suggested. Ironing takes up more space, but there is no absolute necessity for an awkward freestanding ironing board.

Many of them are unstable at best, and hard to set up and fold away. A wall-mounted board, a board that slides out from a counter, or even a small countertop board all take up far less space. Note that any built-in board must be located so that when the iron is plugged in, the cord is not in the way of the ironing.

Broom closets, often found in a laundry or utility room, can be the perfect place to locate a fold-out ironing board. The board itself can be attached inside the cupboard or to the inside of the door.

Supplies

At every stage of the laundry process there are many supplies that need to be kept near at hand—detergents, stain removers, bleaches, fabric softeners, starches, anti-static sheets, and perhaps dyes. These items are best kept shelved above the area where they will be needed, along with the iron and ironing cloths. Another solution is to use a cabinet, either wall-mounted or built under the laundry sink, if there is one. It may also be possible to construct triangular shelves to fit into the corners created by the washer and dryer and the wall in back of them, and take advantage of the space at either side of the machines. If you build laundry equipment into a niche, with a surrounding system of cabinets, keep in mind that you will occasionally have to get at the backs of the machines for repairs and maintenance.

Shelving for supplies may also be made to support hanging clothes by the addition of a row of hooks under the front edges of the shelving.

Not strictly related to laundry but often associated with it is a sewing and mending center. Unless this is a major pastime, a box or drawer somewhere in the laundry room can usually be found to accommodate enough equipment to sew on buttons and effect minor repairs in material. Moreover, this is also a good place to store leftover lengths of curtaining and other fabric that has been used around the house. All that is needed is an extra shelf or a small amount of space in a closet.

If sewing is an actual hobby and a sewing machine is involved, then something more elaborate is called for; a filing-cabinet-size container is not a difficult project for the person who is handy. If it's on wheels, it can be rolled away out of sight or under a countertop when not needed. Project 13 shows a simple sewing center (see page 148).

THE UTILITY ROOM

Either combined with the laundry room or as a space in its own right, a utility room is a wonderful asset. No matter how small a space, you need somewhere to store all the things needed to run the simplest household, even the household of a determined *non*-do-it-yourselfer. It can be no more than a simple shelving system at the side of the basement stairs or a single closet in a passage or hallway.

At the most basic level, every house should be equipped with a hammer, a screwdriver, and a pair of pliers. Usually, this is just the beginning of a collection of tools. Most households also keep a few extra light bulbs on hand, a minor example of the things that contribute to the well-oiled running of the house. These do not properly belong in the main rooms of the house and are stored most conveniently in the utility area, whether a room or not. The utility room often functions as the laundry room, as discussed earlier. But even if your utility room is simply the space under the stairs, next to the fuse box, taking the time to assess its contents and organize the storage space will help you use it efficiently.

Cleaning Supplies

Perhaps all that is available to serve as a utility room is a broom closet. This term has gone far beyond its literal meaning to include all kinds of cleaning aids and appliances. There may be small brooms, dustpans, mops, dusters, rags, floor sponges, buckets, pails, scrub brushes, and a host of cans and bottles containing cleaning powders, liquids, and polishes.

After making sure that the tallest item you possess—usually a broom—has room to stand up, install shelving in the rest of the closet.

Hang the broom, and other long-handled items such as mops, on spring clips or hooks behind the door or under the shelving. Hang up as many other items as possible, from the back of the door, the walls, and the shelves themselves.

If your space is larger than a mere broom closet, apply the same principle; hang up as much as possible, and you will discover more space and remain better organized. Long-handled items are best arranged like garden tools in a garden shed: Bore a hole in the end of each handle and hang the collected items from a row of nails. Some can even be hung upside down between a pair of nails.

Buckets, pans, and pails may be nested if necessary, but avoid the temptation to use them to store other objects, which only creates confusion and clutter when they are needed.

Most vacuum cleaners come with numerous attachments these days. Sometimes these are stored in the housing of the vacuum cleaner itself, but often they're not. Try to create a permanent home for these attachments or they'll disappear without a trace just when they're needed. Allocate or construct a shelf somewhere for these parts (and for extra bags if needed), and life will be easier.

The utility room or area is similarly the best place for small rechargeable vacuum cleaners, as well as rechargeable flashlights. These units can generally be attached to the wall (provided there is an outlet nearby into which they may be plugged). It's worth the effort to do so, rather than allowing them to take up valuable shelf space elsewhere.

Industrial-Strength Cleansers

Sooner or later we all accumulate something a little stronger than the typical household cleanser. Often these are highly potent and may contain toxic chemical material, such as ammonia or chlorine. Here the key word when considering storage is safety. Flammable materials should be kept outside the house, if possible. In any event, keep them in sealed metal containers, safe from inquisitive children and pets and inadvertent breakages and spills. Solvents, varnishes, urethanes, and even paints should be handled with similar care. Rags and brushes used with these materials are usually best thrown away rather than saved, but even the disposal of them must be done with care. Rags used with linseed oil, for example, can self-combust if not stored in an airtight container or kept under water. If such things must be kept in the utility room, you should locate a fire extinguisher there.

Tools and Supplies

Sooner or later, you'll go beyond the hammer, screwdriver, and pliers previously mentioned and you'll acquire many other odd tools and gadgets. All of these will probably be very useful, provided they are kept where you can find them, preferably in a simple toolbox with compartments. Using even a small fishing-tackle box is better than allowing these items to disappear into the back of a drawer.

As a general proposition, don't mix tools with hardware and supplies. Avoid the temptation to throw those extra screws and lengths of picture wire into the toolbox. Keep the toolbox for tools and provide a separate box or container for small hardware. It's usually hopeless to hunt for a replacement washer for the kitchen at the bottom of a toolbox amid a jumble of tools and hardware. If you enjoy accumulating odd bits of hardware, keep them sorted in separate glass jars, which allow the contents to be seen without having to be emptied out. Another alternative for a collection of nuts, screws, washers, and bolts is a small multi-drawered cabinet. Each drawer should hold only one type of item and be clearly labeled.

Homeowners also tend to build up a collection of items unique to their houses, such as tiles left over from a bathroom renovation, lengths of carpet, plant hangers, flower pots, extra panes of glass, and lengths of screening. Think carefully about all these items. Some are irreplaceable and so are truly indispensable—like the extra piece of carpeting, which cannot be bought again. But unless you are an inveterate and active do-it-yourselfer, it may make sense to throw some of the items away and use the space for something else. Most are readily replaceable at the hardware store, and you are rarely likely to need more than one or two. The occasional expenditure may be a price worth paying for less clutter and more space for something truly useful.

Emergency Supplies

Apart from fire extinguishers, there are one or two other emergency items that the prudent householder should keep at hand. Depending on which part of the country you live in, you may want to keep one or two self-fueled heaters in the event of a winter power outage, a supply of drinking water and some canned food for a possible earthquake emergency, and candles and flashlight wherever you live in case the electricity is interrupted. All these items must be stored so that they are easily and instantly accessible, possibly in the dark. A box of candles stuffed into a small space at the back of an under-stair cabinet or in the freezer compartment of the refrigerator is *not* good storage. Keep them where they can be found logically by almost anyone.

7

PORCHES, ENTRANCES, STAIRS, AND HALLWAYS

Unless a large and grand residence is concerned, we generally give little thought to entrances, halls, and passages in a home. We tend to think of our houses in terms of the rooms described in the typical real-estate listing: bedrooms, bathrooms, kitchens, and so forth. Even in a small apartment, however, there is usually more to the place than the actual rooms. There might be, for example, a front and/or back entry area, perhaps a porch (possibly enclosed), a main entrance hall or foyer, stairwells and landings, hallways, and other odd corners, ells, and niches not strictly part of any particular room.

Many of these can be adapted for all sorts of storage, either for items that belong to a specific room or area or for an overflow of items for which the original space is simply too small. At the same time, it is surprising how many things actually *do* belong in these areas, umbrellas by the front door, for example, but for which we often fail to make sufficient provision.

PORCHES AND ENTRANCES

If you have a front door (as opposed to a shared apartment entrance), the addition of a porch, no matter how small, is a great convenience. Even a small overhang over the door will provide a measure of weather protection for callers and yourself. Extend or expand the porch projection into something a little larger, and a wealth of possibilities opens up.

66

With a full roof and a couple of posts supporting it at the front, seating can be built between the posts and the door. By boxing in the seats, you can create storage for anything from snow shovels to muddy shoes. Depending on the size of the porch, which in turn depends largely on the size and style of the house, you can fit out quite a spacious and comfortable area. It might be big enough to keep several people protected from the weather, store packages and garden tools, and include such conveniences as boot scrapers and message racks, along with proper protection for doorbells, mailboxes, and intercoms (see figure 7.1).

Most city houses—and some in the suburbs—have front entrances that are used as their main entrance. But many country houses, as well as many suburban houses, are approached by a driveway leading to an attached or detached garage. Although visitors may still approach the *front* entrance, the occupants may well use the *side* entrance, because it is more convenient to the driveway. Furthermore, such houses sometimes have additional entry

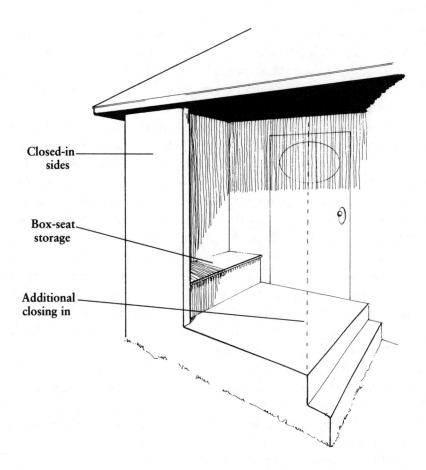

Figure 7.1   Front-porch storage

porches or verandas at other places. These extra entrances, which often see more use than the front entrance, can be a hidden asset to those with special storage problems.

A large back porch not only provides all the storage possibilities of the front porch, perhaps to an even greater degree, but it can also be the ideal place for bulky or awkward items that you want to keep near but not in the house. Firewood in a rack, containers of kindling, pet supplies, grocery carts, bicycles, scooters and skateboards, and strollers and baby carriages can all be kept there.

If the porch is open, you'll have to decide what is safe to keep and store there; if it's enclosed and provided with a lockable door, then the choices are much greater. Ideally, some or all of the items listed would find a more appropriate home in a basement or garage (see chapter 9, "Basements," and chapter 10, "Garages"), but that is not always possible.

Entrance Halls

Whether you enter by the front door or a second entrance, there are many items whose use will begin or end at that door. It makes sense to house them there, if possible, to ease the storage shortage elsewhere. Items such as hats and coats, gloves, scarves, mufflers, umbrellas, walking sticks, and perhaps galoshes or rain boots, ought to have a home here.

Whether you adapt these storage devices to the front or back entrance will depend on the use that either receives. It obviously makes more sense to provide most accommodation at the entrance that is used most frequently.

The old-fashioned hall stand, often an imposing and handsome piece of furniture, has much to commend it (although it is not compatible with all types of decor). As a single unit it can lend focus to an entrance as well as provide a place for many of the things that you might want to keep there. Not only can hats and coats be hung, but racks for umbrellas with drip-catching trays are often provided, as well as a mirror for those final adjustments just before leaving or just after arriving (see figure 7.2).

A coat tree is somewhat simpler, though less commodious. It is still better than nothing. Although both the hall stand and the coat tree might not be suitable for every location, they can fit easily in a space too small for a separate closet. Even a row of coat hooks can help relieve overcrowding in the bedroom closet, if it's doubling as a coat closet. You can almost always find *somewhere* to place a coat hook or two, or even a row of them—behind doors, in corners, on the outside of closets, either side of doorways, even under the stairs.

You'll also need drawer and/or shelf space for items like gloves and scarves. If a closet isn't available or practical to build, consider freestanding pieces

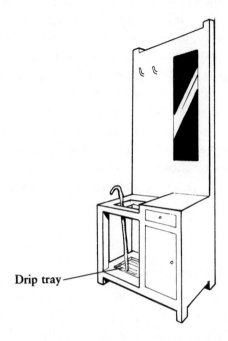

Drip tray

Figure 7.2   Hall stand

such as small wardrobes or chests of drawers. You can also use large crocks or baskets for umbrellas. There is often room in an entrance for such pieces. Besides storage, they can add a spark to an often boring space.

Since entrances are often very irregular areas, with doors and passages leading off at all points, there can be many oddly shaped spaces. You can sometimes build shelves or shelving units to fit into these odd stretches of walls or unused corners and niches. Very often there is room above the doorway for a wide shelf that can perhaps be enclosed with doors or curtains to keep seldom used but bulky items such as suitcases and other articles of luggage.

One more piece of furniture that should be considered is the hall table. Small or large, it is always very useful to have a surface on which to put things when coming in from outside. A table with drawers can also provide a place for small items such as gloves, sunglasses, maps, lists of restaurants, and other such paraphernalia.

STAIRS

Wherever a staircase exists, it may be a source of much potential storage. Even if the staircase is closed off, the space below it can often be opened up to house cabinets or shelves. The secret of maximizing this space is to build the shelving so you don't lose things in the farthest recesses down at the floor level; you don't want to get down on hands and knees to reach anything. If possible, try to make the access from the side rather than from the end (see figure 7.3). In such an installation, shelving is built across the back of the space rather than under the actual treads.

No matter how you build shelves under the stairs, remember that it may sometimes be necessary to reach the under-side of the treads and risers—the actual stairs—for maintenance of some kind. One way of ensuring future access is to use trunks or chests of drawers rather than built-in shelving. If these are equipped with wheels or casters, they will be more accessible. You can wheel them out into the open where you'll have more headroom to deal with them.

The various flights of stairs, the runs of steps and landings that progress from floor to floor, may also yield some storage space. Instead of open balusters or bare walls along the stair, consider adding shallow shelving or cabinets. Of course, safety on a staircase is paramount, and you should never restrict the width in a way to jeopardize that. Usually, however, there will be sufficient width to use the space at least on one side.

Consider the landings carefully. Again, you have to be careful not to

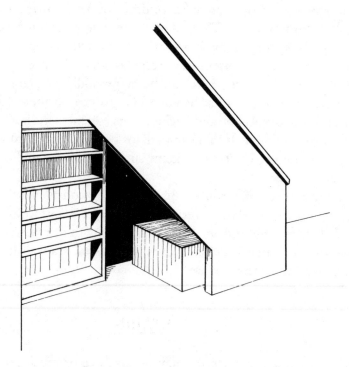

Figure 7.3   Under-stair storage

compromise safety. Nevertheless, there is often room on a landing for a bookcase or corner cupboard. With a certain amount of ingenuity, the space over a landing or stairwell can be put to use. By lowering the ceiling height—often a simple matter of fixing ledger strips around the opening a certain distance below the existing ceiling, and framing out a simple platform with a side door or trapdoor access—a kind of extra attic is created, which can be used to store all manner of items. Project 14 (see page 152) shows how such a storage space is created.

A more ambitious project involves turning the risers, which are the vertical parts of a staircase that support the treads, into drawers. Since this involves rather complicated carpentry affecting the structure of the staircase, it should be attempted only by someone experienced in construction. But if properly done, it can transform a flight of stairs into a kind of chest of drawers.

HALLWAYS

A final source of space, outside of the rooms per se, is in the various hallways. If suitably lit, perhaps with an added skylight, and furnished with mirrors at strategic points to increase the impression of space, the hallways can become more than the "nonspace" they frequently represent. They can take on a life and purpose of their own.

Lining their walls with bookcases or pictures is a simple expedient. But equally appropriate is to use them for display cabinets for china or glassware. Such cabinets do not need to be very deep, and, if built with glass-paneled doors, they can add much to an otherwise dull area.

Where two or more corridors intersect, the construction of floor-to-ceiling shelving or closets can sometimes help define the area to better advantage. It might even afford one of the rooms some extra privacy. You can also build a closet or wall-width shelving system in the dead ends of a passage.

One advantage of creating extra storage space in hallways is that almost anything may be stored here with equal justification. A suitably enclosed freezer can make just as much sense as a freestanding piece of antique furniture.

8

THE ATTIC

The attic has traditionally been considered the ultimate domestic storage area, the place for things not needed on a day-to-day basis. The very word conjures up visions of heirlooms and forgotten treasures moldering in dusty and disorganized gloom under the rafters, just waiting to be discovered by the next generation.

Although there is something to be said for creating this kind of grab bag for those who may follow us, most people cannot indulge in such a luxury today. Few families now stay in the same house for very long, let alone for several generations. In addition, attics tend to be smaller and space for necessaries is too precious.

Nevertheless, the attic—even the smaller attic of today—can still be a prime storage area for today's increasingly transient population, provided certain preparatory steps are taken. These include not only better organization (so all areas are accessible) but also attention to the physical condition of the attic, which can bear on the "health" of whatever we store there.

ASSESSING THE CONDITION

The condition of an attic depends largely on whether it is finished or unfinished. An unfinished attic may have problems of ventilation, condensation, and insulation, which can adversely affect whatever is stored there. A finished attic usually has some sort of floor and, often, a covering on the rafters. A finished attic that has been turned into active living space is no longer really an attic, yet problems just mentioned should still have been addressed if this area is to be suitable for people or storage.

Before the recent emphasis on energy conservation, the attic presented few problems as a storage area. Typically uninsulated, it was well ventilated as a result. It might have been blisteringly hot in summer and frigid in winter, but it would nevertheless have kept things dry and relatively safe. Moreover, older houses tended to have steeper roofs and therefore more space under the rafters.

This has all changed. Insulation is everywhere. Though indisputably essential, insulation nevertheless creates a few problems, especially in attics, that did not previously exist.

First, the insulation itself can be harmful to health if improperly installed. If an attic area is to be used at all, loose insulation must be covered. Some insulation consists of potentially harmful material that must be properly shielded. Behind walls and in ceilings it is fine, but when encountered loose, lying between the joists of an unfinished attic floor, it constitutes an unacceptable hazard.

Second, insulating an area usually goes hand in hand with sealing up all air leaks and gaps in a building. The joints around windows and doors are tightly caulked, and building paper and impermeable membranes (called vapor barriers) are used inside walls and ceilings. As a result, the house gains in thermal efficiency but becomes subject to the problems created by inadequate ventilation. These sometimes can include the inadequate venting of toxic gases and other substances, produced both naturally—as in the case of radon—and by building materials such as formaldehyde. More usual and less threatening to health, but just as devastating to the structure, are effects of condensation caused by lack of ventilation.

As a result, any attic space intended for storage should be carefully inspected. If the house has been well insulated, you'll probably find that it needs a certain amount of finishing before it will be suitable either for you or for the items to be stored.

Insulation

No insulation should be exposed, whether it's in the form of paper-backed or foil-backed fiberglass batting, loose fill insulation, or rigid board insulation.

It's quite common in an attic to find loose insulation spread between the ceiling joists of the room below (see figure 8.1). To use the attic at all, you'll need some form of flooring over these joists. You can put weight safely only on the joists, not between them, or you run the risk of breaking through the

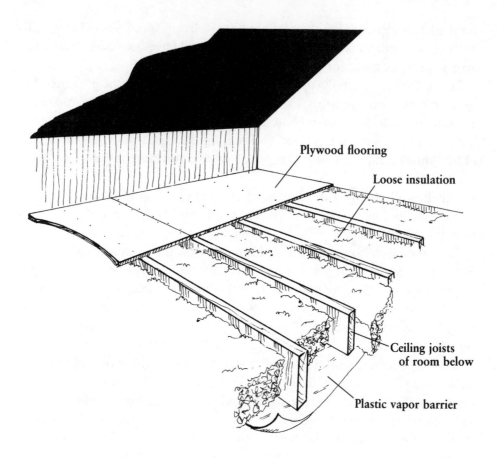

Figure 8.1   Attic flooring

ceiling below. A few boards or a sheet of plywood laid across the central area can create a sort of catwalk, but it won't give you much storage space and will leave large areas of insulation exposed. It is better to seal the entire surface with a continuous floor. It need not be a finished floor; any surface strong enough to support your weight and that of the intended storage will do. Sheets of plywood or particleboard are the quickest materials to use, but ordinary boards may be necessary where space is tight.

If there is insulation exposed between the rafters in the "wall-ceiling" of the attic, this should also be covered by a continuous skin of foil or plastic. If not, you'll have to install sheets of plastic. Overlap the sheets and seal the joints with tape.

The aim is to seal the occupied area from any contact with the insulation material. At the same time, however, it's important not to interfere with any ventilation systems that may exist. These are ridge vents, soffit vents, or open spaces designed to allow the passage of air between the exterior of the building and the insulation. If this air flow is insufficient, under the right conditions, condensation can severely damage the structure itself and its contents. Thus, when a previously uninsulated area is sealed, provision must be made for proper ventilation. Since this involves technical considerations, you should seek the help of a professional.

Other Considerations

Undoubtedly, the main living areas of a house should be insulated in order to conserve the energy necessary for heating or cooling. In the attic, however, it may not be necessary to insulate the actual roof, provided you're aware of the possible temperature extremes that might occur. Even in mild areas of the country, uninsulated attics can become extremely hot in summer; many stored items might suffer under these conditions.

Ideally, you might want to finish the attic so you could store anything there, regardless of the climate. But it may not be worth the effort. Many attics are not well proportioned for unrestricted access. Headroom may be a problem; access to the lower eave space may be difficult. There may be many structural members, such as trusses, collar beams, and posts, which can constitute serious obstacles, and complicated exterior roof lines, hips, dormers, and gables can all add up to odd-shaped areas inside. You should not attempt to modify, remove, or replace any of these structural features without the advice of an expert. And when done just for storage purposes, such modification is often not justified.

STRUCTURAL IMPROVEMENTS

Despite the warnings just given, there may be much you can do structurally to make any given attic more suitable as a storage area. Apart from providing a full floor, probably the most important aspect is access. If you're lucky, you'll have stairs to the attic already; they may well be narrower and steeper than your main staircase. Sometimes, especially in older houses, the flight of stairs leading to the attic is behind a door. This can be a problem unless the door is easily removable, because the door may impede your moving large items up the stairs. Loose pin butts (hinges with a removable pin) are desirable.

If there are no attic stairs, access may be through a small hatch or trapdoor in the ceiling, there primarily for inspection purposes. The opening is invariably too small and too difficult to reach to allow you *and* anything other than the smallest items through. The best solution is to enlarge this opening and install a folding staircase. If this is not possible, a ladder attached to the nearest wall may at least make it easier to enter the attic. But if the attic is to become a good storage area, the entrance must be enlarged so that you can move things in and out. Project 15 (on page 157) shows how to enlarge an attic opening.

Having created a proper access to the attic, the next thing to consider is lighting. This may mean installing a simple lighting circuit. Depending on the size of the attic, it may mean no more than providing one fixture operated by a pull chain close to the entrance. For a larger or more complete job, you may want to have an electrician install several strategically placed fixtures so that all parts are well lit.

Walls and Ceilings

Since shelving is more easily built against vertical walls than on sloping surfaces, and since the area at the bottom of the roof is so hard to reach, knee walls can greatly improve an attic of any size. A knee wall is simply one that extends from the floor to the sloping roof rather than to a full overhead ceiling. Knee walls in an attic increase the vertical wall area at the cost of very little usable floor space. Even that space can be made available through doors built into the knee wall, which turn the space behind the walls into cupboards (see figure 8.2).

An allied idea is to partition off any space too small or awkward to use. A very simple partition wall made with two-by-four studs covered with wood, plywood, or gypsum board (see figure 8.3) will define the area and give you a wall for shelving or racks.

Of course, by the time you have improved the entrance, built staircases, insulated, added light fixtures, laid floors, made walls, and installed ceilings, you may find that you have created a whole new space suited to more than just storage. One note of caution: your building code may have restrictions, for example, on available headroom, the proportion of window to floor space, and overall building height, which govern any space used for living purposes. It would be wise to check the applicable codes first.

Assuming nothing is proscribed by law, many attics, especially with the addition of a dormer or a skylight, can indeed be turned into extra rooms— for children (who do not need high ceilings), for guests (for whom headroom is not crucial during a short stay) or even for yourself (an office, for example, where there is at least sufficient room to sit at a desk). Deciding where to draw the line when improving the attic may be the hardest part.

Figure 8.2   Knee wall with doors

ITEMS FOR STORAGE

Perhaps nowhere in the house is it harder to be ruthless about what should be stored and what discarded than in the attic. This is, after all, the place for things about which we are unsure. Yet the same basic rule applies here as elsewhere: "Less is better." But if a few principles of organization are followed, we may find room for more storage than we had thought.

First, avoid loose storage, especially of small items. Keep things in boxes or containers, and label these boxes and containers clearly. If it's worth keeping, it's worth keeping where it can be found easily. A well-labeled series of boxes—either home-recycled cardboard boxes or specially designed folding boxes from a stationery or office-supply store—can be stacked up along one wall in far less space than the unboxed contents would occupy.

Second, plan for proper preservation of the stored item. Attic storage is typically reserved for things that may not be needed for very long periods of time. Depending on the object and how perishable it is, make provision

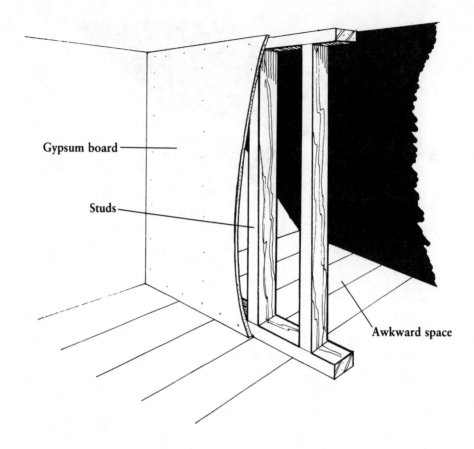

Figure 8.3   Attic partition wall

to protect it from dust, moths, rodents, and deterioration caused by exposure to light, heat, or cold.

If an item is not worth taking the time to pack, wrap, seal, enclose in a dustproof container, mothproof, rustproof, or whatever else may be applicable, it probably should not be given a home in the attic. It should either be disposed of or kept elsewhere.

Mementos

Sentiment can justify anything. Rocking horses, childhood toys, school souvenirs, and military-service mementos are typical of the miscellany found in an attic. Some of these defy regular packing or sorting, and an occasional inspection is necessary to forestall deterioration. If you see or even suspect moth damage, leave a few mothballs or camphor sticks around. If rust threatens metal objects, use rustproofing paper for wrapping or apply a light coating of rust inhibitor. To kill off woodworm or other insect infestations, seal the suspected item in plastic and freeze it for a couple of days. If rodents such as bats, rats, mice, or squirrels threaten to eat into your storage, screen or seal up possible entrances, use traps, or practice natural control (get or borrow a cat).

Paperwork

Paper materials are among the most perishable and demand rigorously controlled conditions if they are not to deteriorate rapidly. Unfortunately, modern living creates many paper items that we feel compelled to keep, such as financial records, checks, receipts, income-tax statements, as well as many we want to keep, such as letters, souvenirs, books, magazines, and photographs.

Storage conditions are extremely important. Paper will deteriorate rapidly if exposed to light, moisture, heat, or poor ventilation, and can also be destroyed by insects of all kinds. Although most contemporary paper items are made from stock that is not acid-free, thus effectively condemning them to dust within 50 years or so, there are steps you can take to ensure the maximum lifetime.

Try to keep the temperature between 60 and 75° F and the relative humidity between 50 and 60 percent. Avoid exposure to light, but provide sufficient ventilation. A dry, moderately warm place with good air circulation is best. Keep paper items in boxes so that they are protected from the light, but do not seal the containers so that mold can develop. If moisture is bound to be present, include a packet or two of silica gel to absorb it.

If the environmental conditions are as good as they can be, give some thought to organizing paper storage into different classes. Properly organized file cabinets, letter files, document holders, and other specialized containers will make access easier and actually hold more than makeshift shoe boxes or other salvaged containers.

A shelving system like a large bookcase is ideal for boxed paper storage and can be set against any convenient wall, as long as the wall is insulated. Small filing cabinets can make efficient use of the space under the rafters. They can be built into a knee wall so that only the drawer fronts are visible.

Not everything is recorded on paper anymore. Film, tape, and computer disks are but three nonpaper forms of records that are increasingly common. Unfortunately, these too are relatively vulnerable. Light, heat, moisture, and magnetic fields are the enemies here. Archivists go to extraordinary lengths to preserve irreplaceable documents, but the precautions outlined above should be sufficient for common household records.

Clothing

Provided there is sufficient protection from dust, moisture, and insects, the attic can be an ideal place to store out-of-season clothes. Two excursions to the attic a year can make all the difference to overcrowded bedroom closets. Hanging clothes bags, which provide excellent protection from dust and insects, can be used; they can be hung easily from lengths of closet rod fixed between rafters in unfinished attics (see figure 8.4) or suspended in a more orthodox fashion from finished walls or ceilings. To avoid moth damage, clothes should be hung in garment bags. There are also hanging shelf units made of fabric or clear vinyl, sized for shoes and other small articles.

Even simple built-in closets should be considered. Anything closed, however, should be provided with vents, suitably screened to keep out insects but still allow air to flow. Chests and trunks are equally useful. You might also consider movable hanging racks, especially if they have protective covers.

Soft Furnishings

Some items can be stored only in the attic. They are really too large for any other room in the house, and basement or garage storage might not be

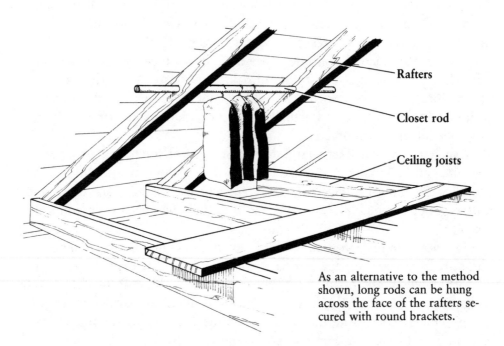

Rafters

Closet rod

Ceiling joists

As an alternative to the method shown, long rods can be hung across the face of the rafters secured with round brackets.

Figure 8.4   Closet rod in attic

sufficiently safe. Such items include carpets, drapes, quilts, extra mattresses, and bedding.

Carpeting should always be stored rolled, never folded, and preferably around a core, such as a large cardboard tube or wood dowel. Although it should be wrapped to protect against dust and insects (include mothballs), there should be air circulation. Thus prepared, a carpet may find a home in the rafters, resting on collar beams, or rolled away under the eaves.

Other fabric items may be stored similarly, but avoid the use of plastic wrapping, since many natural fibers need to breathe to maintain their resiliency. If fabric is stored folded, it should be refolded periodically in a different direction to prevent permanent creases. Arrange such items on shelves rather than stacking them on one another.

Mattresses should be protected with covers, then stored vertically against walls or partitions. Use boards or sheets of plywood to keep them vertical and prevent them from slumping. If stored flat, keep them off the floor, up on a simple pallet.

Furniture

Moisture and insects are the worst enemies of furniture stored for a long time. If you can protect against these two evils, the attic can safely house almost any furniture. A dust cover should be used over large items, such as tables, that can be safely stored only in their natural position. Smaller items, such as chairs, can very often be hung up out of the way, perhaps on a row of pegs or spikes on the wall.

9

THE BASEMENT

In general terms, a basement refers to the lowest level of a building, when sunk at least partially below ground. It need have no specific purpose other than its structural role as the base of the building. The older term "cellar," on the other hand, which originally referred to a storeroom located anywhere, is now used primarily for a room excavated *below* a building and designed specifically for storage. In our discussion, we'll use the term *basement* for all such spaces.

Some houses, such as those built directly on a slab foundation (see figure 9.1), simply have no basement storage. At the other end of the scale is a house with a full and improved basement. Such a basement may have finished walls, floors, and ceilings, and sufficient headroom (the term *full basement* implies at least 6½ feet floor to ceiling) to walk upright in. There may well be windows, if the basement walls rise above grade, a proper entrance from the inside down a flight of stairs, and even an outside entrance. Such a basement may constitute a finished living space, and as such be used as a family room or a recreation room.

Older buildings were very often built on basements excavated to a certain depth, with the space enclosed by dry stone walls laid up against the raw earth. Depending on the customs and conditions of the area, a floor may or may not have been installed.

In between these two extremes exists an endless variety of lower-level spaces, more or less finished as the case may be. Some are so small that they constitute no more than what is called a "crawl space." If the building is

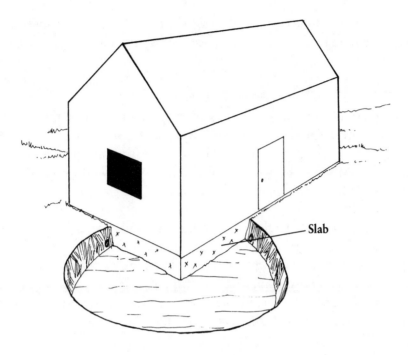

Figure 9.1   Slab foundation

supported not by a perimeter wall enclosing a subterranean space at all but by a series of posts or stone pillars, it is said to have a "pier foundation." Such minimal spaces, often open to the elements, are not very valuable for storage purposes (but see page 88).

ASSESSING THE CONDITION

Obviously, within such a range of possible structures, conditions will vary greatly; the basement may well need certain improvements before it can be used for storage of any kind. Some basements may have been designed for a now out-of-date storage purpose, such as a root cellar or a coal cellar, and may be difficult to convert to modern uses.

Some more recent houses, even those provided with full basements, have these areas left largely unfinished, for reasons of economy. The spaces may well be cut up by the "works" of the modern house: the furnace and ductwork, the electric service box with its snarl of wiring, pressure tanks, hot water heaters, and other plumbing necessities. All of these can present problems when planning for storage.

As a result, a basement area may well need more preparation than any other area of the house. Nevertheless, since the basement usually extends under the whole house, it can comprise a substantial area worth improving.

Dampness and Moisture

Because there is often only a porous concrete floor, because the water table is so close to the surface, or because drainage from the roof or outside the building is poor, the basement can be anything from merely damp to decidedly wet. Few things fare well if stored under such conditions; the problem should be identified and corrected if possible.

High water table.   If the floor is wet but the walls are dry, it is likely that the problem is from ground water seeping up through the floor. Installing a properly waterproofed concrete floor is the only permanent solution, but cost may make it entirely impractical. If the problem is not continuous and manifests itself only after heavy rains, it may prove more practical to install a sump pump to deal with the temporary flooding whenever it occurs.

Leaking walls.   A more common cause of basement moisture is water leaking through the walls. Ideally these should have been built to be completely waterproof, and today many building codes do require various waterproofing measures. Older buildings may not be so fortunate, especially those constructed with stone walls laid up dry (without mortar joints). If the leak is not too serious, it may be possible, with the help of various waterproofing patching compounds, to seal the wall from the inside. If the leaking is serious, the best approach is to deal with the source of the water rather than try to waterproof the walls. This involves excavating the ground around the outside of the basement walls, a major undertaking.

Among the most common sources is water that runs off the roof and, because of clogged or broken gutters and downspouts, is not led *away* from the foundation. Another common source is water that runs down outside slopes and is not properly drained *away* from the foundation of the house.

The cure for gutter problems is obvious: proper maintenance of gutters and downspouts, and attention to draining their flow away from the house. At least twice a year, clear all leaves and debris from the gutters and check that the strainers at the top of the downspouts are in good condition. Make sure that water will flow from the farthest end of every gutter to the downspout end, and that the downspouts themselves are both unobstructed and so designed that they will empty at least eight feet away from the building.

If the land around the house is improperly graded, laying new drains

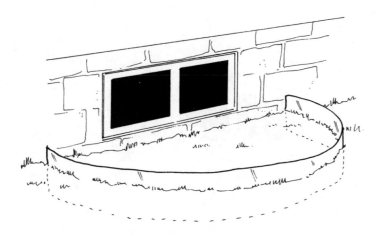

Figure 9.2 Basement window flashing

around the perimeter of the house may solve the problem. This is a major operation, however, since it can involve excavation down to the bottom of the foundation and proper siting and sloping of perforated drainpipes in a bed of gravel. At the very least, the grading should be improved, ensuring that the surface slopes down and away from the house at all points. Pay attention to flower beds that abut the foundation; prevent any pooling of water in them.

Another culprit in this area can be leaky or improperly protected basement windows, which allow water to flow in during heavy rains. Very often all that need be done is to install a small barrier—a 12-inch strip of metal flashing is ideal—around the perimeter of the window well (see figure 9.2), though a properly constructed concrete or steel window well is best (see figure 9.3).

Condensation. A damp basement can simply be the result of excessive condensation, caused by warm interior air meeting the cold surfaces of un-insulated walls and cold water pipes. To determine whether basement moisture is the result of condensation rather than leaking, tape a 6-inch square of metal or metal foil to the wall. If, after a day or so, the metal is wet on the wall side, the problem is seepage through the wall; if the metal is wet on the room side, condensation is the cause. (It's possible that both conditions may pertain.)

If the problem is indeed condensation, insulating the walls will prevent moisture from forming on them. Once the basement becomes a little warmer,

Figure 9.3   Concrete basement window well

however, the cold water pipes are likely to sweat even more. If there is a good deal of such piping, you should wrap it with insulating material and seal that with a vapor barrier. Special pipe-jacketing material is available at hardware stores and lumberyards precisely for this purpose.

Other measures for minimizing condensation include improving the ventilation by using fans, opening (or even creating) a window, and installing a dehumidifier.

Moisture problems in the basement must be solved one way or another if you are to use it for any real storage.

The Right Temperature

Far less important than moisture problems is the question of temperature. The level of warmth maintained in the basement will depend on what you intend to store here. Cold storage is often a plus for certain things. For other items, it is always possible to make the basement warmer. Windows can be double-glazed or fitted with storm windows; walls can be insulated and finished; and the heating system can be changed to provide some extra heat to the basement. Project 16 (see page 160) shows how to insulate basement walls.

Since furnaces are often located in the basement, the provision of an extra length of ducting fitted with a register open to the basement itself is usually a relatively easy operation.

If both warm *and* cool storage areas are needed, consider partitioning off part of the basement, to accommodate both temperature ranges.

Spatial Arrangement

Assuming you have resolved the problems of moisture and temperature, consider the way the basement is arranged. There may be little logic to the placement of the various utilities; the units may have been installed wherever seemed most convenient at the time.

Within reason, almost anything can be moved, although you may need a plumber and an electrician to do it. With a few moves, a surprising proportion of the area might be opened up to provide good access and usable storage. Furnaces, however, are best left in position, since they are often very large units installed on their own slab or foundation. Have a conference with your plumber or heating contractor to discuss what you'd like to do. If the house has had several electrical upgrades over the years and has more than one service box, call in the electrician and discuss consolidating the web of wiring and boxes into a safer, more convenient system.

More recent houses may require only surface treatments, such as wall finishing and better lighting. In some cases, you may be able to improve the access to the basement.

So far we have been talking mainly about full basements, but some areas that are less than "full" can still offer storage facilities. A crawl space, if made accessible by the provision of a short flight of steps instead of a trap-door, or by an opening from the outside, can be useful. Some basement areas combine a full basement with a crawl space, especially if the house is built on sloping terrain. It may be possible to extend the crawl space by a certain amount of excavation, but before you try this, get the advice of a qualified builder or architect.

Taking the opposite approach and restricting the area may also make sense. By partitioning off an unusable area and finishing the remaining space, you may be able to create a proper, safe area for storage, protected from the creatures and conditions that might be prevalent in the unfinished area. If you do this, however, be sure that you provide for access to the unfinished area if it contains water pipes, sewage lines, heating ducts, or other vital components.

As you prepare the basement for storage, consider fire safety: check for possible hazards such as exposed wiring and insufficient clearance around furnaces and electrical appliances. Consider installing a smoke detector and a fire extinguisher in the basement.

Insect damage is the other major hazard to consider in a basement or crawl space that is likely to be less finished and consequently more exposed than other areas. Make periodic inspections of all exposed wood for telltale signs of insect infestation, such as little piles of sawdust (indicating beetles or carpenter ants) or fresh entrance holes or tubes possibly caused by termites. An annual inspection by a qualified agency is the best way to prevent damage not only to the house but also to the stored items.

SHELVES, RACKS, AND BINS

There is virtually no end to the list of items that might be stored in the basement. It can serve as an overflow for other areas in the house, as well as provide storage for items that can find no home elsewhere. As an adjunct to the kitchen, the basement is ideal for preserved and canned food. Part of the basement can be used as a wine cellar. It can double as a utility room and laundry room, providing a place for washing machines and workshop items, as well as emergency supplies. It can even hold garden supplies, especially if there is an outside entrance and you are not lucky enough to have a garden shed at your disposal. Furthermore, there is no reason why at least part of the basement may not serve as a room in its own right—a den, game room, study, or hobby room.

Even crawl spaces under houses built on piers can be used for wood storage or garden supplies, especially if made secure from animals by the installation of a screened entrance. Wood storage requires a special word of caution, however: keep the area clean and be sure to use the wood in rotation. Don't leave a section unused for a long time, since stacked wood presents an invitation to all kinds of insects that might easily make their way into the house itself.

Shelving and Racks

If the basement walls have been finished, attaching or building shelves and racks should present no greater difficulty here than in the rest of the house. But if the basement area still has the original unfinished masonry walls, the procedure is a little different.

If you're dealing with a block wall and need a secure anchor, it is always preferable to attach something to the masonry itself rather than to the mortar

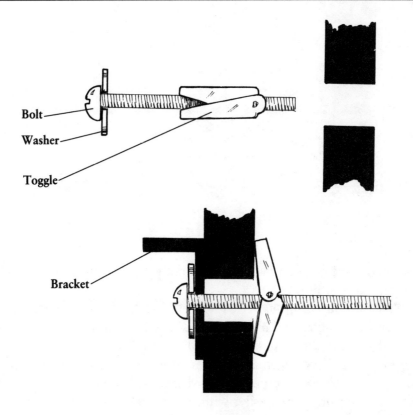

Figure 9.4   Toggle bolt

joints between blocks. If you're dealing with a brick wall, a whole brick can be removed and replaced with a wooden block, known as a noggin, to which screws or nails can be attached.

Attaching anything to masonry will usually require drilling. Always wear some form of eye protection. The exact type of fastener will depend on the kind of masonry involved. There is a large range of fasteners available at a good hardware store; a clerk should be able to help you select the right kind.

Concrete blocks, being hollow, require either very short plugs or some form of toggle bolt. To install a toggle bolt, drill a hole just large enough to allow the folded wings of the toggle bolt to be pushed through. As you do, the wings will open up and allow you to draw them back tightly against the interior surface of the wall (see figure 9.4).

Plugs, or expansion anchors, are made of various materials, including plastic, fiber, or wood types for relatively lightweight construction, or metal fittings if heavier objects are to be attached to or hung from the wall. In either case, drill a hole the same diameter as the plug, making sure it is deep enough to contain the plug completely, then hammer in the plug. Inserting

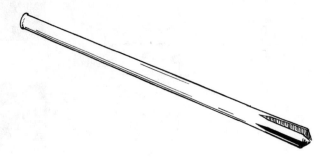

Figure 9.5   Star drill

a bolt or screw into the plug forces it tightly against the walls of the hole and creates a firm fitting.

Drilling the hole is done either with an electric drill using a special masonry bit or with a hammer and a special cold chisel called a star drill, which is given a slight turn after each hammer blow (see figure 9.5).

Another alternative, when attaching anything to a masonry wall, is to use masonry nails. These are especially hard steel nails that are driven in either with a hammer or, more easily, with a cartridge-powered stud gun. This tool can be rented from hardware and rental stores and is useful for attaching wood studs or furring strips to masonry walls. Make certain you learn how to operate the stud gun safely; you should be able to get instruction at the store from which you rent it.

Ceiling-Hung Units

If the ceiling of the basement is unfinished with the joints of the floor above exposed, you can attach hanging racks (see figure 9.6). Simply nail vertical supports to the sides of the joists, then attach crosspieces to these supports. Such racks can be designed in various sizes to hold many things conveniently off the floor.

Bins and Cabinets

Simple bins with hinged lids are another useful storage facility for basements. These have the advantage of providing discrete and safe storage in basement areas not completely finished or secure from the outside.

Cabinets built against the wall can be useful for items that do not require any special temperature control but must still be protected from other po-

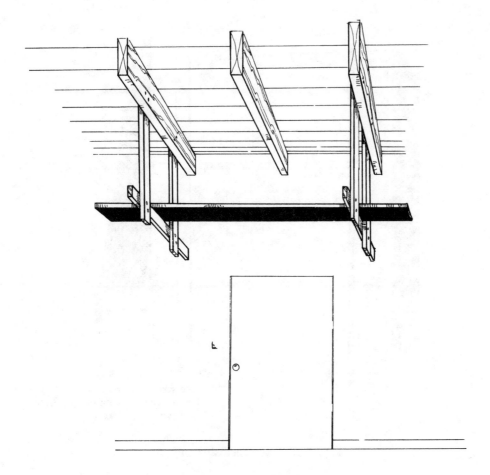

Figure 9.6   Ceiling-hung racks

tential problems, such as mice. Shelving units provided with a removable screen front can accomplish the same thing (see figure 9.7).

The stairs that lead into the basement from above can provide a ready-made framework for extra shelving or closet space, as can the walls at either side of the staircase (see figure 9.8). However, don't narrow the stairs too much; they are often narrow to begin with. Large items such as a replacement water heater may occasionally have to be accommodated.

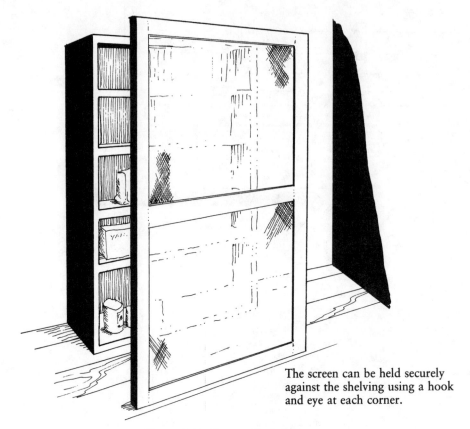

The screen can be held securely against the shelving using a hook and eye at each corner.

Figure 9.7   Screened shelving

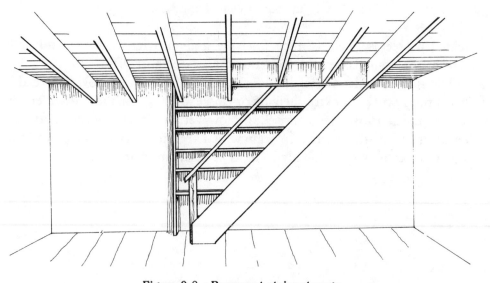

Figure 9.8   Basement stairs storage

10

THE GARAGE

We think of the garage as being the place where the automobile is kept, but for most people the automobile is only a part of the story. (We don't go to garage sales to buy a car!) Indeed, the word *garage* comes from a word that originally meant simply "shelter." For most of us that's exactly what the garage is, our biggest shelter, or storage space.

Aside from the car, the garage is also likely to be home to bicycles, motorcycles, strollers, sports and garden equipment, and numerous other bulky items, such as snow tires, that can't find a home in the house proper. It also commonly serves as laundry room, workshop, and a place for garbage and firewood storage. But even though the average garage is already a warehouse under another name, it is often grossly underdeveloped in terms of storage. With a little planning it can usually be turned into a much better facility.

ADDITIONS AND IMPROVEMENTS

The typical garage is very often little more than an unfinished shell, whether attached or freestanding. As such, it's ripe for improvement. In a way, this is a blessing, since you can custom-adapt it to fit your personal storage needs. Even the humble carport, originally designed simply to protect your vehicle from the weather, can, by virtue of its simplicity, become more useful than you might imagine.

Unlike attics and basements, which are frequently used to store items sensitive to temperature and humidity, garages tend to accumulate a lot of things that are relatively unaffected by climate. As a result, insulation and heating are not usually necessary. More often than not, the garage is raw space, with unfinished walls and no ceilings. Because of this basic simplicity, it could easily turn into a disorganized mess. Even a few basic steps can prevent this. At the very least, a row of nails from which to hang things, such as a few garden tools or the snow shovel, is necessary. A compartmented shelving system on one or more walls will be even more useful. Project 17 (see page 163) shows three ways to attach such shelves.

Most garages have a concrete floor, which usually needs little improving. The lighting, however, is often poor. For a truly efficient storage area, you may want to have a better lighting system installed. In addition, there are many possibilities for modifications and additions that we'll discuss as each kind of storage is considered: lofts, lean-tos, sheds, overhangs, and all sorts of interior bins, bays, and racks.

CARS AND OTHER VEHICLES

Even though the car may have to share the garage, it is still likely to be its biggest occupant; as such, it will occupy pride of place. But while it may take up a lot of floor space, not all of the car extends to the ceiling. This makes possible very deep cabinets or shelving installed halfway up the wall at the front of the car, allowing it to nose in underneath (see figure 10.1).

Of course, anything can be stored here, but it is the obvious place for car-related items that you don't want to carry in the car all the time. Snow tires, spare wheels, coolers, maps, and items that are needed only on long trips should not take up everyday trunk space. They are much better kept stored in the garage on such a shelf. Dedicated mechanics will, of course, want to use part of the garage for tool storage and perhaps even a workbench.

Bicycles can be among the most frustrating objects to store since they stick out and tend to roll away or fall over. Rather than let them take up valuable floor space, install large, plastic-coated bike hooks, available at most bicycle shops, from which they can be hung neatly. In a multi-bike household, space can be saved if adjacent bicycles are hung from alternate wheels, with the handlebars of one bicycle next to the saddle of its neighbor, rather than having all handlebars in a row. Another solution is to stagger the hooks. Whereas several bicycles usually have to be hung at right angles to the wall, a single bicycle may be hung directly on the wall. Instead of hooks, brackets of metal or wood can be used. If you are averse to hanging, consider a floor

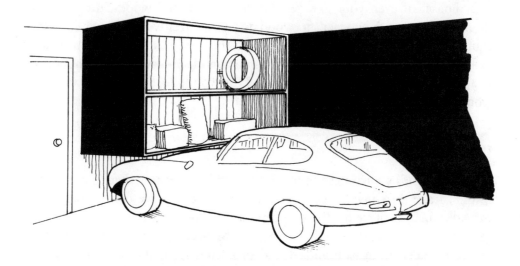

Figure 10.1   Deep shelving over an automobile hood

rack in which one of the wheels can be parked so that the bicycle is kept upright and in place.

Larger items, such as strollers, wheelchairs, snowmobiles, and snowblowers, may be difficult to fit into the garage but can very often be housed in a small closet or lean-to built on the outside of the garage, where they are protected from the weather. If the lean-to is enclosed and lockable, these items are also protected from theft. Project 18 (see page 166) illustrates the construction of a simple lean-to.

FUEL AND WASTE

For many people who burn firewood the garage may be the best place to store wood. If you can enter the garage directly from the house, a wood bin in the garage can be a great convenience on a winter night. The wood bin must be accessible, but it must also keep the firewood contained, preventing it from spilling out into the garage.

If there is no room in the garage for the wood bin, the solution may be to build a wood bin against the outside of the garage. Covering it with a roof is better than nothing. In addition, if you can enclose it, perhaps with a clear plastic roof or a glazed, south-facing wall, you'll have a storage area that also helps dry out and season the firewood.

There are a couple of warnings to heed when storing firewood. First, it is part of nature's plan that dead organic material should decompose with the help of insects and fungi. You do not want to introduce these things into your house, or even your garage. Wood is wood, and wood-eating insects do not discriminate between firewood and structural wood. Check logs for signs of insects before bringing them into the garage, and try not to bring in sawdust with the wood. Keep any inside bins clean—sweep them out once in a while—and allow ventilation around the woodpile. Keep the wood away from the walls a little, and off the ground.

Household Trash

Trash cans are a sometimes unpleasant fact of life. Keeping them out of sight in the garage does help somewhat, but it is better to face the problem and provide a proper place for them. A separate enclosed space inside or outside the garage, not too far from the kitchen or the street, and in a well-ventilated area, will keep things organized and protected from the depredations of dogs, cats, and raccoons. Keeping the cans or bins on a small platform fitted with wheels or casters can ease the chore of carrying these often-heavy items to the curb for collection.

Recycling waste is becoming increasingly common. This typically involves sorting out the various types of garbage, which require separate storage of some kind. The days of one giant plastic garbage container are numbered. Instead, a series of compartmented bins, each separately removable, for paper, metals, plastics, and other rubbish is likely to become the norm (see figure 10.2).

SUPPLIES AND EQUIPMENT

Garden and Yard

Even if limited to indoor plants, the garden can involve a lot of tools, pots, and bags of soil, not to mention larger outdoor equipment, such as garden chairs and tables. Nothing can take the place of a separate garden shed, but if the garage has to serve as home for all these things it should be made as efficient as possible. One small step is to put up a one-by-three across an entire wall, high enough so you can hang up all the long-handled tools. Space the nails and hooks along it for specific tools; drill holes in the ends of the handles if necessary.

By building a small bench in one corner for potting operations, space will automatically be created underneath for bags of potting soil and fertilizer. At the same time, shelves for smaller things such as pots, pruning shears,

Figure 10.2   Sorted trash

and watering fixtures can be built above. Hoses are best hung on a wall-mounted rack near the faucet to which they are attached. The revolving-wheel rack is a great improvement over the standard one, which simply provides a place for the hose to be hung. Sprinklers and watering accessories can often find a home in small, wall-mounted cabinets, which need be no more than a simple wood box or crate attached to the wall.

Large but lightweight items, such as aluminum garden furniture, can be stored on racks hanging from the garage roof, rafters, or walls. Heavier pieces of equipment, such as lawnmowers, spreaders, rollers, and snow-blowers, will need their own floor space.

Sports and Recreational Equipment

Patio furniture, barbecue grills, skis, tennis racquets, badminton nets, and countless other items connected with leisure pastimes all find their way into the garage, this being the most logical storage place for them, especially out of season. Some of these, skis, racquets, and bats, for example, are small and light enough to be hung up. There is, after all, usually much more wall space than floor space, and they will fare better when they are not underfoot.

For more awkward items, shelves may be better. For seasonal equipment such as toboggans, sleds, or golf clubs, shelves above doors or high up will leave more accessible areas free for everyday things.

Really large items, such as camper tops, canoes, surfboards, and wind-surfers, can often be hauled up and suspended from the ceiling or roof, or kept in specially built overhead racks.

A word of caution about garden or patio cooking supplies: it is always risky to keep flammable materials such as charcoal briquets and lighting fluid in the house. These items should be stored in sealed metal containers and kept in well-ventilated, childproof places. A separate metal cabinet or bin is a good idea. The same is true for fuel supplies for lawnmowers and other powered garden equipment.

Do-It-Yourself Supplies

No house should be without a stepladder, but this is a large and awkward object to have standing around. Hanging it horizontally from brackets or hooks inside or outside the garage is convenient, but you may also consider sliding it over the collar beams in the garage roof, if yours has them.

Other handyman supplies, tools, and equipment are more useful the better separated and more easily accessible they are. A heap of tools and assorted hardware left over from previous jobs, jumbled up in a box in the corner, is discouraging when you come to the next household repair. As mentioned, keep tools separate from hardware and supplies; you'll find yourself more willing to reach for them when needed. The same principle holds true for all sorts of supplies, from nails and screws to pieces of wire, hooks, hangers, and tape. If you store these items in separate containers (in glass jars or cans on a shelf, clearly labeled) and gather paints, solvents, spackle, and other supplies together in a cabinet or cabinets, you'll be able to find them when needed. That's the only way they'll be of any real use.

Tools themselves can be hung from pegboard, housed in simple wooden racks, or even attached to magnetic wall strips. Small plastic bin units are ideal for screws and fasteners. Larger self-stacking trays are best for bigger items.

All this should be considered basic equipment for every house. Very often, however, a larger work area will be needed. For the enthusiastic do-it-yourselfer, a workbench can often be constructed along one wall of the garage. This not only provides useful working space but also suggests storage possibilities over and under the bench—for example, shelves, cabinets, or perhaps a floor-to-ceiling cabinet at one side of the bench. Project 19 (see page 169) shows how to build a simple workbench.

HOUSEHOLD OVERFLOW

Inevitably, if there is a garage available, there will be extra paperwork, surplus clothing, mementos and souvenirs, as well as many other things that will find their way into it. If these miscellaneous items cannot be thrown away, you may be able to find storage space for them in the garage without jeopardizing the garage's basic functions. If you're faced with this problem, make good use of cabinet and box storage, and if possible, roof storage.

Depending on how the roof is constructed (and often on what kind of garage door or doors you have), it may be possible to put a plywood floor up on collar beams that reach from wall to wall in many garages. But be careful not to build anything that interferes with the operation of an overhead door. This kind of loft storage space can be created even if there are no collar beams. Attach ledger strips to the side walls as high up as possible, then connect them with beams, and lay down the plywood (see figure 10.3).

Since garages are typically unheated, they serve well as overflow pantries and even wine cellars. If wine is a special interest, note that the large, cool area of a garage, which is often built with few windows, can be an ideal location for wine racks and bins. It is also a natural place for extra canned supplies and preserves.

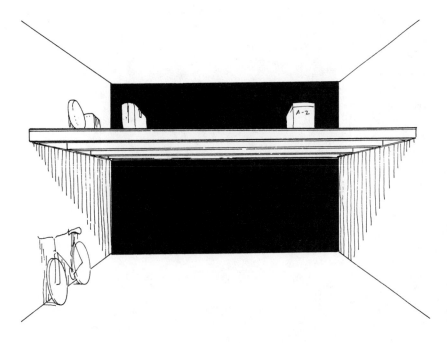

Figure 10.3 Garage loft storage

PART II

Storage Projects

PROJECT 1

A Basic Bookcase

The simplest way to make a basic bookcase is to use standard-size boards direct from the lumberyard. This will eliminate the need for much cutting. In fact, if you plan the few components carefully enough in advance, most lumberyards will be happy to cut your boards to the right length ready for assembly.

The board most useful for bookcase construction is known as a one-by-twelve. The actual measurement of the board, however, is about ¾ inch thick by 11½ inches wide. It may have been a full inch thick and a full 12 inches wide when it was originally sawn from the log, but the processes of seasoning and making it smooth will have reduced it. Except for material sold in sheets, such as plywood and particleboard, all lumber is somewhat smaller than its "nominal size," unless it is specially marked. Measurements of length, however, are usually exact, if not a litle generous.

One-by-twelve boards will make shelves deep enough for the majority of books. The next size down, one-by-ten, will hold all but large art books; smaller sizes will really hold only paperback-size books. If you need shelves even deeper than 11½ inches, it will be necessary to join boards or use sheet material such as plywood.

In its most basic form, a bookcase needs only the two sides, as many horizontal shelves as you think are necessary, and some form of back. The back may be made of simple diagonal braces of one-by-two or, far better, a full back made from ¼-inch plywood. No matter how well you join the shelves to the sides, you cannot omit the bracing, or back, or the bookcase will lack stability. With a full back nailed to the back of the bookcase, the joinery can be of the simplest kind and the bookcase will still be stable and sturdy.

The only practical limit to the height is the height of the ceiling in the room the bookcase is intended for. Width is a different matter. Shelves made of one-by-twelves, loaded with books, will sag if much longer than 3 feet. A full back that is nailed not only to the sides of the bookcase but to the shelves as well, will make the shelves stronger. But if you're building a bookcase wider than 3 feet, it will be necessary to provide uprights every 3 feet or so.

The basic bookcase should be built with fixed rather than adjustable shelves unless you're skilled enough to tackle a more complicated building problem. Don't try to space the shelves for your tallest book; you'll inevitably find at least one other book that is taller. Decide on a spacing that will house the majority of your library and be content to lay the very tall ones on their sides. A height of 12 inches will accommodate most books.

With this in mind, make a rough sketch showing the height and width of the proposed bookcase, and draw in the shelves the required distance apart (see figure P1.1).

The easiest way to join the shelves to the sides is to make sure the ends are cut perfectly square and nail through the sides into the ends of the shelves. You must be careful to position the shelves accurately and hold them in place while you nail. Mark the position of each shelf beforehand in pencil (see figure P1.2). Center the shelf on the pencil line and nail, using 2-inch finishing nails.

If you have access to any kind of power saw, or a router with a straight bit, you can make grooves (called dadoes) across the insides of the sides, into which the shelves will fit (see figure P1.3). Dado construction will not only make the shelves stronger but will also make it easier to get the shelves fixed at the right height, assuming you lay out the dadoes carefully. One of the secrets to cutting proper dadoes is to cut both side pieces at the same time, thus ensuring that the shelves are set into each side at exactly the same height. (The technique for laying this out is shown in figure P3.2, page 115.)

Whether you simply join square boards or use dadoes, there are two refinements that will make a better job. The first has to do with the top. Instead of setting the top *within* the sides as you do the other shelves, make the top the full width of the bookcase including the sides and nail it *down* onto the sides (see figure P1.4).

The second refinement has to do with the bottom of the case. Cut a piece of one-by-two to fit under the bottom shelf (see figure P1.5). The bottom

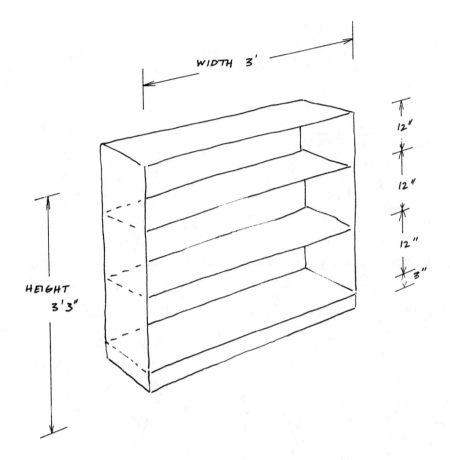

WIDTH 3'

12"

12"

12"

3"

HEIGHT
3' 3"

Figure P1.1   Rough sketch of proposed basic bookcase

shelf will then be raised up, so you'll have to adjust the height of the other shelves to compensate. But you'll have a better-looking and more stable bookcase. Instead of resting on a slightly warped bottom shelf that could cause the bookcase to rock or wobble, it will now rest more securely on the three edges formed by the two sides and one-by-two at the front.

Fitting the back is the final job. Plywood is made in sheets 4 feet wide by 8 feet long, and it's best to cut the back out of one sheet, if possible. You can join plywood pieces at the shelves if necessary, but it will be easier, and make a stronger case, to cut (or have it cut at the lumberyard) a single sheet to fit the exact size of the back.

Nailing the back on (see figure P1.6) will not only make the bookcase rigid but will also ensure, if the plywood has been cut to size with perfect right angles, that the sides are plumb and the shelves are level. How-

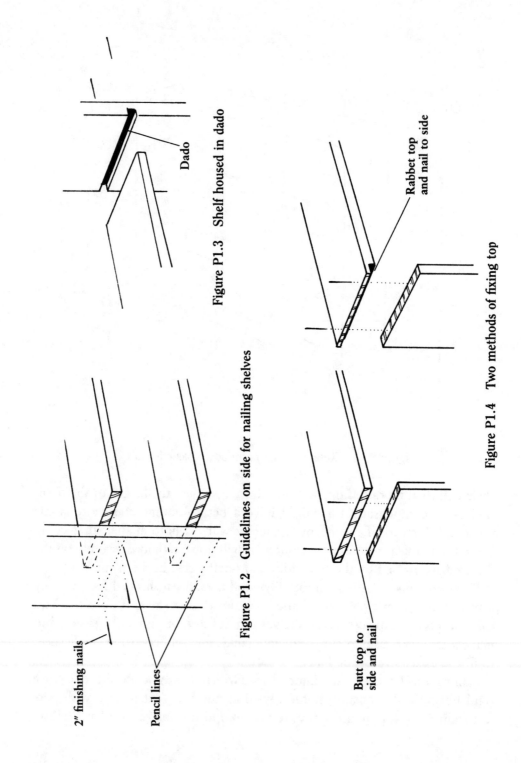

Figure P1.3 Shelf housed in dado

Dado

Figure P1.2 Guidelines on side for nailing shelves

2″ finishing nails

Pencil lines

Rabbet top
and nail to side

Butt top to
side and nail

Figure P1.4 Two methods of fixing top

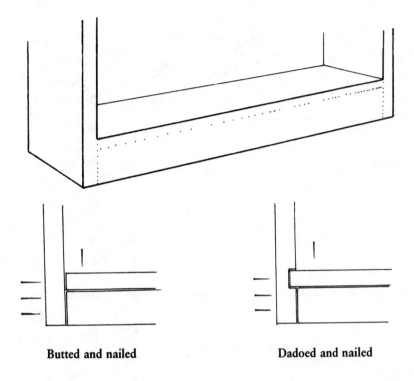

Butted and nailed   Dadoed and nailed

Figure P1.5   Two methods of fixing base at front

ever, if the floor where it is to stand is not level, you'll have to attach the
case to the wall or provide some form of leveling, with shims, for example.
It is far better to level the case than to try to fit the bookcase to a sloped
floor.

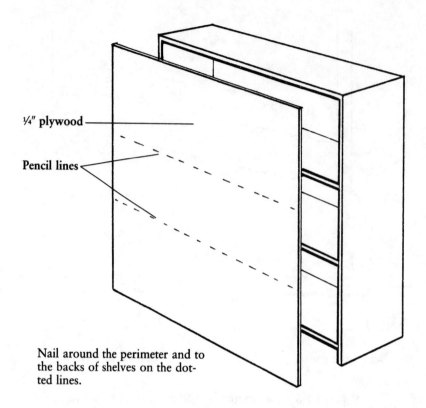

¼" plywood

Pencil lines

Nail around the perimeter and to
the backs of shelves on the dot-
ted lines.

Figure P1.6   Attaching a back

PROJECT 2

A Basic Entertainment Unit

With so many different entertainment components available—not to mention storage space for the items, such as tapes and discs, used by the components—it is virtually impossible to design a unit that might be applicable in all situations. Whatever you build should be able to be adapted to changing requirements for individual components, and should provide maximum storage for audio- and videocassettes, long-playing records, and compact discs.

The basic entertainment unit shown (see figure P2.1) can be built in such a way that, with a little planning, it can be modified to suit individual requirements. Essentially it is a large, two-piece cabinet, easily constructed using cabinet-grade plywood for the most part and requiring only a few tools.

The bottom half is designed to house speakers at each end and provide storage for tapes, discs, and records in the center. The top half will accommodate a TV set and a separate VCR, as well as the other components in your hi-fi. Within the structural limits explained below, the actual dimensions can be adjusted to suit your requirements.

Begin with the bottom half. Using ¾-inch plywood that has a good surface on both sides (ask for "good two sides"), cut out the two sides, as seen in the exploded drawing (figure P2.2). A depth of 24 inches is sufficient to hold many televisions and most speaker cabinets but may be increased if necessary. The height of 30 inches may also be adjusted if required, but this should be adequate for most speakers. It will also hold two rows of long-playing records and provides a comfortable counter height for the top cabinet. Note the

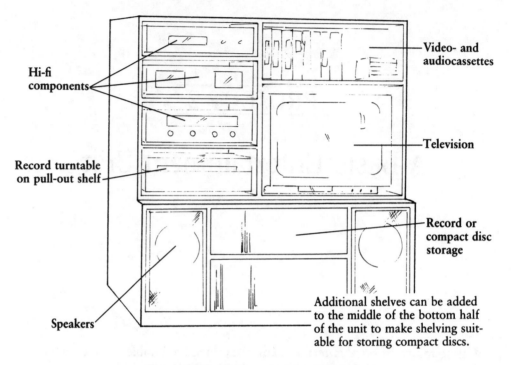

Hi-fi components

Video- and audiocassettes

Television

Record turntable on pull-out shelf

Record or compact disc storage

Speakers

Additional shelves can be added to the middle of the bottom half of the unit to make shelving suitable for storing compact discs.

Figure P2.1   Basic entertainment unit

small cutouts at the bottom of the side pieces. These are designed to receive a base strip, measuring one-by-two (¾ by 1¾ inches), the length of the cabinet. It can be cut from the same plywood or simply be a length of one-by-two.

The top and bottom pieces are the same depth as the sides, but the bottom piece is 1½ inches shorter in length than the top piece, since it fits *inside* the end pieces whereas the top piece goes *over* the ends. The exact length of these pieces will be determined by the space the cabinet is to occupy and by how wide a cabinet you want to build. Anything much longer than 4 feet, however, will require extra support to prevent sagging.

Screw the top to the two ends first. For a neat job, drill pilot holes, use 1½-inch wood screws, countersink them, and fill the holes with wood filler. Next, attach the bottom (off the floor as shown) to the two side pieces, screwing into the bottom through the sides. Attach the baseplate with screws. Then measure the inside height for the two partitions (the depth is the same as the sides) and cut them out, securing them in place by screwing through the top and bottom. Make sure that the compartments created at each end are wide enough for your speakers.

Now attach the back. Make it from ¼-inch plywood and attach it with

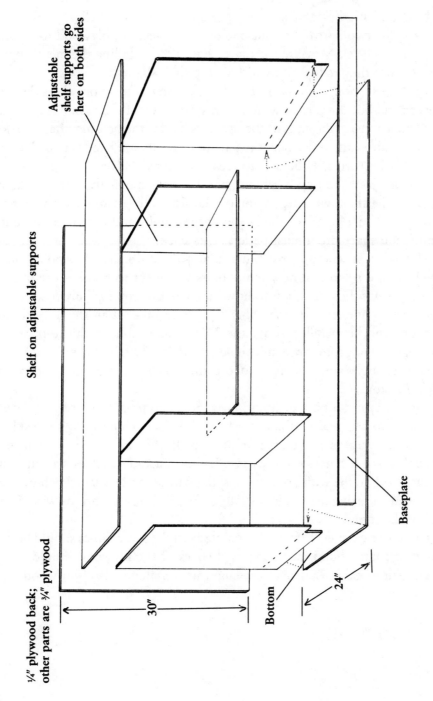

Adjustable shelf supports go here on both sides

Shelf on adjustable supports

¼" plywood back; other parts are ¾" plywood

30"

Bottom

24"

Baseplate

Figure P2.2   Exploded view of bottom piece

small nails. If this piece is cut with perfect right angles, it will ensure that the cabinet is properly square.

Last, attach adjustable shelf supports (metal strips or clips) to the inside faces of the two partitions. Cut one or more pieces of plywood to form the shelf (or shelves). Measure for the shelves *after* installing the metal support strips, since they reduce the width of the shelf slightly.

The top section is similarly constructed, first cutting out the sides, then the top and bottom pieces, which in this case are both the same length, since both attach inside the ends of the uprights. Screw the box together as before, then measure, cut, and attach the partition. A full-size back is nailed on. Use shelf support strips, as before, to create as many shelves as necessary.

The depth of the upper cabinet may be the same as the bottom cabinet, or it may be shallower, depending on the size of the components you intend to house. The TV set is usually the deepest unit, and a certain amount of ventilation space often must be left at its back.

The height of the upper cabinet is also discretionary, depending on the height of the room and how many units you want to house. Bear in mind, however, that there is a limit to how high you can comfortably reach to deal with the components. If the cabinet is to be taller than the TV set, shelf supports can be installed above the TV set, as well as in the compartment to its side. (That compartment can be on either side, of course.) If the cabinet is wide enough, you can create two compartments for components or tape and disc storage.

Since it is important to house electronic equipment securely, it may be advisable to secure the cabinet to the wall by screwing through the sides or the back, using an angle iron at the top. If you do this, be sure to leave enough space behind for the wiring. If the adjustable shelves are cut a little shallower than the width of the sides, the wiring can be snaked behind them. A few judiciously bored holes usually suffice to lead the various wires in and out of the cabinet.

Before the cabinet is stained or painted, all the screw holes should be filled smoothly; large holes in the exposed edges of the plywood should also be filled with wood filler. Cover the edges with matching iron-on wood tape.

PROJECT 3

A Basic Display Shelf

The principles behind this piece are quite simple and can be adapted to many types of display units. The shelves are dadoed into the sides, and the unit is attached to the wall by means of a horizontal ledger strip that has been notched into the backs of the sides (see figure P3.1).

Dadoing the shelves into the sides simply means that the ends of the shelves

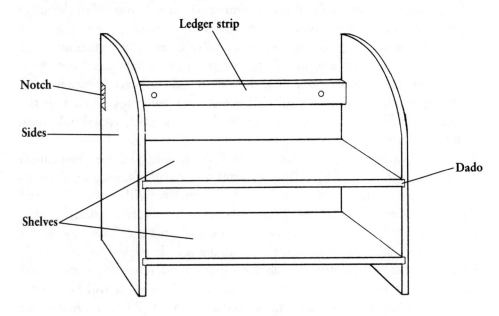

Figure P3.1   Basic display shelf

are fitted into grooves (dadoes) cut in the inside faces of the sides. This is an extremely secure way of making shelves and enables them to carry maximum weight safely. The secret to its success lies in fitting the shelf ends nicely into the grooves.

The ledger strip by which the unit is attached to the wall illustrates the other main building principle involved in this piece. Because the strip spans the entire width of the piece, it gives you freedom to attach the piece to the wall at just the right spots (usually at the studs). And because it is notched into the backs of the sides, it can carry much more weight than if it had been simply nailed or screwed to their back edges.

The display unit is thus composed of only three elements: the shelves, the sides, and the supporting ledger strip. Depending on the thickness of the lumber used to make this piece—it might be ¾-inch or 1¼-inch stock—the piece can be a very small unit, perhaps just large enough to hold a few paperback books and a small pot or two, or a much more substantial piece up to 3 or 4 feet wide, with perhaps half a dozen shelves supported at one or more intermediate points. The principles of construction remain the same in either case.

The construction procedure is the same, too. First cut the sides to the desired length. A medium unit might use so-called one-by-six lumber (¾ inch thick). The top ends (and the bottom ends, too) can be rounded off, as illustrated, using a jigsaw. The sides can also be shaped in other ways, but you must leave sufficient wood at the point where the sides will be cut out for the ledger strip.

Next, from the same dimension of lumber, cut the shelves all to the same length. Their actual length will be a function of the wall space you have to work with and of the load they are expected to carry. Many such units are small enough that there is no danger of the shelves sagging. Three feet, however, is about the limit that ¾-inch-thick wood can reach before it starts to sag under the weight of books. Use this as a guide for estimating the potential weight-to-sag ratio. If you want longer shelves, you should plan on intermediate supports.

There are various ways to cut the dadoes, depending on the sophistication of your woodworking skills. Using a router or a circular saw equipped with a set of dado cutters is the fastest way if you have either of these (and experience using them). It is perfectly possible, however, to cut dadoes using simple hand tools: a square, a saw, and a chisel. In either case, laying out the dadoes is the most important part of the job. Having decided exactly where you want to position the shelves, mark the dado cuts on the inside faces of the sides, using a square to ensure that the shelves will be exactly horizontal. Mark both edges of the dado cut (see figure P3.2). To make sure that the shelves are at the same height on both sides, mark the dado cut

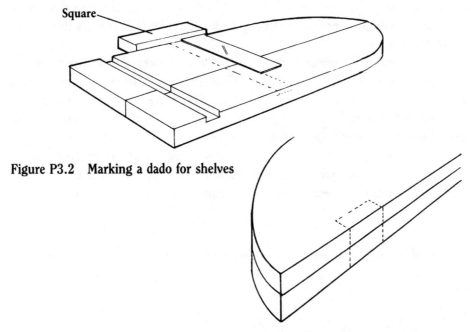

Figure P3.2   Marking a dado for shelves

Figure P3.3   Marking a notch for ledger

across both at the same time, lining them up as shown. Make sure you have both inside faces up and that both pieces are top to top and bottom to bottom.

If you are working with power tools, use the appropriate guides and cut the dadoes to a depth one-third the thickness of the wood. If you are using hand tools, mark the depth at each edge (one-third the thickness of the wood), and use a fine-toothed saw to saw down just inside the marked lines to this depth. The waste is then chiseled out using a chisel the same width as the dado. Chisel out a little bit at a time rather than trying to cut the full depth all at once. If you have worked carefully, the ends of the shelves should fit snugly into the dadoes. But don't assemble the unit yet.

The notch for the ledger strip must now be marked out and cut. Whatever size ledger you are using—a one-by-three will be enough for most medium units—make sure that the notches are exactly the same distance (and no less than 2 inches) from the top on both sides. Mark them (see figure P3.3), then saw down the sides. Make the inside cut with a jigsaw or chisel out the notch. Once again, if you have worked carefully, the ledger should fit snugly in its notches.

Begin the assembly by fitting the shelves into the sides. Put some wood glue in the bottoms of the grooves before putting the shelves in; then nail through from the outside into the ends of the shelves with 1½-inch-long finishing nails (wire nails with very small heads). With a nail set, set the heads just below the surface. Don't mar the surface of the wood with the hammer; that's the reason for using a nail set. Then fill the resulting holes with wood filler.

Use the square to make sure the sides and shelves are perpendicular to each other, then measure for the length of the ledger strip (it is longer than the shelves because it laps over the sides). Then cut it out and attach it as you did the shelves. For even greater strength, use screws instead of nails, predrilling the correct size holes.

Clean up any glue that may have squeezed out (a damp cloth will do it) and apply the finish you've chosen. When it's dry, mount it on the wall, screwing through the ledger strip, preferably into the wall studs.

PROJECT 4

A Typical Window Seat

Building a window seat presupposes that the bottom of the window is high enough off the floor to accommodate a seat below it. It also helps if the window is low enough so that a seat built at normal height (from 15 to 20 inches high) will permit the sitter to see out. It is even more helpful if the window is in a bay, recess, or corner, so at least one wall can form a side of the seat. That also gives the sitter a back to lean against (see figure P4.1).

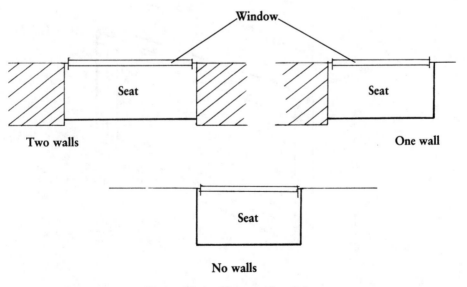

Figure P4.1   Seat configurations

The basis for the window seat is a frame made of two-by-twos, to which the front panel of plywood is attached and on which the front edge of the seat itself rests. The back edge of the seat rests on another two-by-two that is attached to the wall as a ledger. If the window is in a bay or recess, the seat and the front will extend from one side of the recess to the other and there will be no need to make sides.

Decide first on the height of the seat. Make it as close to 18 inches high as the bottom of the window and its trim will allow. Assuming that an 18-inch-high seat will fit, make a frame of two-by-twos with dimensions as shown in Figure P4.2. Note especially that the horizontal pieces extend to the outside of the vertical pieces. This will support the seat better than if the verticals were attached to the ends of the horizontals. Note also that if the height of the seat is to be 18 inches, the height of the frame must be ¾ inch less to allow for the thickness of the ¾-inch plywood that will form the seat. Last, note that the width of the frame must either equal the width of the recess into which the seat is to fit, or if a freestanding seat, be 1½ inches less than the finished width to allow for the sides (two pieces of ¾-inch plywood).

In nailing this frame together, the nails must be driven in very close to the ends of the pieces. As a result, there is a real danger of splitting the wood. To avoid this, predrill holes for the nails, making them just slightly smaller than the thickness of the nails.

Next, cut a two-by-two ledger strip the same length as the frame. Attach

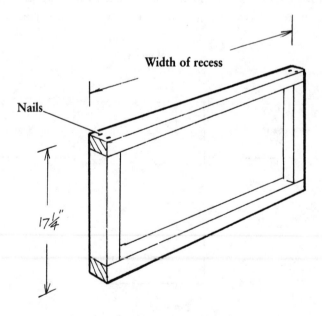

Figure P4.2   Front frame

this to the wall below the window at the same height as the top of the frame. If yours is a wood-frame house, nail it through the wall covering to the studs (usually at either side of the window and, often, below the center of the window). If you're dealing with masonry wall, you'll have to drill holes in it with a masonry bit and insert plugs. Then screw through the ledger into the plugs, using long screws or lag bolts.

If the seat is located in a recess, simply secure the frame to the floor and to the sides of the recess by nailing from the inside (see figure P4.3). If it is freestanding on one or both sides you'll need two-by-two uprights below the ledger strip (see figure P4.4). You'll have to notch the frame to accommodate any baseboard or molding along the bottom of the wall. Once the frame is nailed into position, cut a ¾-inch plywood panel (or panels) to form the side of the seat (see figure P4.5). The top of this panel should be even with the top of the frame and the ledger; the front should be flush with the front of the frame. If there is a baseboard or molding, the panel must be notched out to accommodate it.

The front panel should be cut and attached so it completely covers the front of the frame, from wall to wall if the seat is recessed; if it's freestanding, the front panel should cover the front edges of the side panels. Like the side panels, the front panel should be exactly as high as the top of the frame.

All that remains now is to make the seat panel. If it is a recessed seat, this panel should fill the space completely, less ¼ inch at each side so it will easily

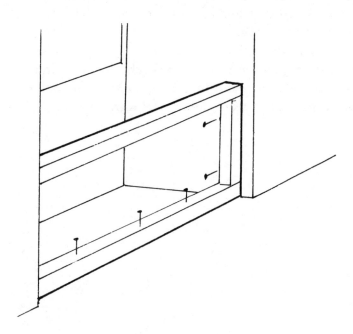

Figure P4.3   Fixing frame in recessed space

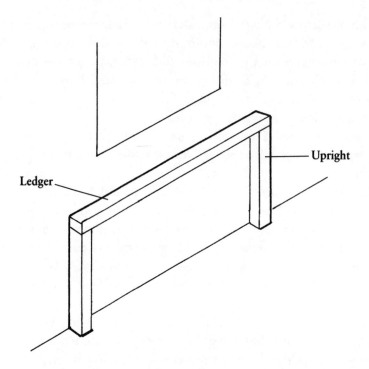

Figure P4.4   Freestanding unit: uprights under rear ledger

clear the walls when removed or replaced. If the seat is freestanding, however, it should overhang the frame by ½ inch at each side. Attach lengths of ¾-inch one-half round molding to the edges of the seat. Use a miter box to miter the corners of the molding.

The easiest way to keep the seat in its place is to attach a narrow strip underneath the panel just behind the back edge of the frame (see figure P4.6). This will prevent the seat from sliding forward; the wall under the window, of course, prevents it from sliding backward.

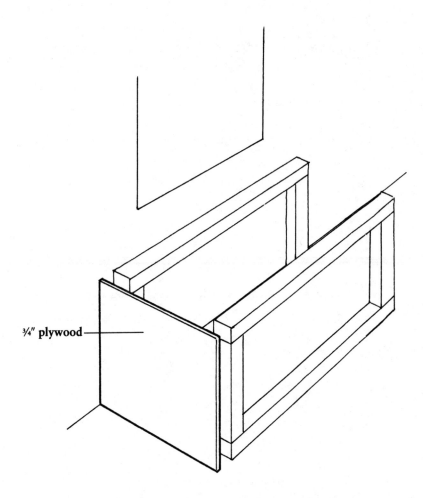

¾″ plywood

Figure P4.5   Plywood panel for open side

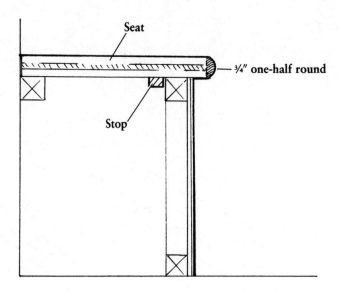

Figure P4.6   Cross section of seat showing stop

PROJECT 5

Drawer Dividers

Here are two simple ways to reorganize drawers: one designed to make better use of a large drawer by dividing the space into separate, adjustable compartments, the other designed to make better use of a small but deep drawer by providing a compartmentalized lift-out tray.

A large, deep drawer is fine for a few large items, but if it becomes home to many small objects, finding a specific item can be time-consuming. On the other hand, permanent divisions keep you from reorganizing as life-styles change. It's best to install dividers that can be adjusted as needed.

Start with two sections of ½-inch plywood cut to fit in the front and back ends of the drawer (see figure P5.1). It is not necessary that they be as high as the drawer ends, but they should fit neatly between the two sides.

In these pieces cut a series of vertical grooves ⅛-inch wide, ¼-inch deep, and approximately 1 inch apart. (The exact distance apart is not important as long as the grooves match in both pieces.) The easiest way to cut the grooves is with a table saw, if you have one. Use a blade that makes a ⅛-inch-wide cut. Another way is to use a router with a ⅛-inch straight bit. A third way is to glue a series of plywood or hardboard strips onto the face of the plywood, each ⅛ inch apart from the next.

These grooved pieces are glued into the ends of the drawer (see figure P5.2). The dividers are made from ⅛-inch hardboard and cut so they fit neatly into the grooves. Make as many dividers as you need and insert them into the grooves that create the compartments you need now. Don't glue them in; you may want to change them in the future.

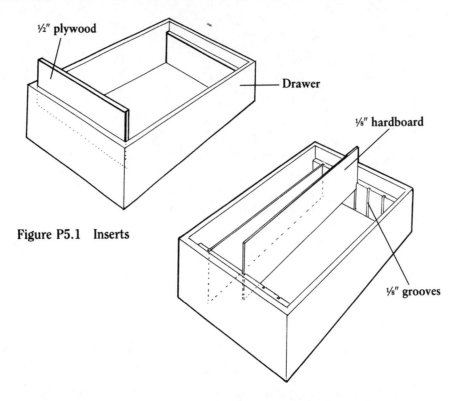

Figure P5.1   Inserts

Figure P5.2   Dividers

In a small but deep drawer the idea is to create a second layer of storage on a lift-out tray. To support the tray, you line the inside faces of the drawer with strips of ½-inch plywood (see figure P5.3). These pieces should be half the depth of the drawer. If you cut and fit the side pieces first, you'll only have to attach the two end pieces, since they will hold the side pieces. You can use short nails or screws, but white glue is probably easiest. You don't need much glue, but clamping each end after gluing will help.

To make the lift-out tray, start with a piece of hardboard, finished smooth on both sides, ⅛ inch smaller all around than the inside measurements of the drawer (above the strips you've just put in place). This will be the bottom of the tray, which will rest on the strips. Pieces of ½-inch plywood form the sides of the tray. Make sure that the four sides are exactly the same height (a little less than the distance from the ledge in the drawer to the top of the drawer). Butting the ends (see figure P5.4) is the easiest way to join them. Note that the ends are the same length as the tray bottom, but the sides are shorter by as much as the thickness of the ends. Cut the ends first, then put them in place in the drawer and measure for the sides.

Before gluing and nailing the sides together, decide whether you will want any partitions in the tray. If so, make the appropriate grooves as in the

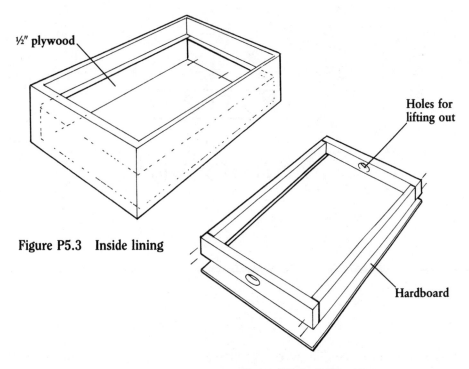

½″ plywood

Figure P5.3   Inside lining

Holes for
lifting out

Hardboard

Figure P5.4   Lift-out tray

partitioning project (see figure P5.2). Last, bore a 1-inch hole in the center of each end (or each side if there is a partition in the way), so you can easily lift the tray out of the drawer.

Glue and nail the sides together, but predrill the nail holes in the ends of the sides or you'll risk splitting the wood. Plywood is more resistant to this than solid wood, but it is still a wise precaution and a good habit to get into. Last, nail the bottom to the tray frame, using many small finishing nails.

If you're dealing with a deep drawer, you may want to make a tray that is only half the length of the drawer. If you do that, you won't have to lift it out every time you need something from below; you can simply slide the tray forward or backward.

PROJECT 6

A Serving Cart

Once you understand how the serving cart goes together, you can easily modify it to include more levels or fit different dimensions. It is made with ¾-inch plywood ends and shelves, one-by-three solid-wood shelf supports, and one-by-six solid-wood shelf edging.

Taking time to plan how best to cut the different pieces from the sheet of plywood will not only save work but will ensure that you make maximum use of the material. For example, assuming the dimensions to be as shown in Figure P6.1, the best way to divide a sheet of four-by-eight plywood would be as shown in Figure P6.2. (Making the dimensions exactly 2 feet by 3 feet would not allow for the thickness of the saw cuts in the plywood.)

In the example shown, the sides and shelves are all the same size, so they can all be cut at once without regard for marking them as separate pieces. Having made these pieces, cut six pieces of one-by-three exactly to the width of the plywood pieces (1 foot 11 inches). These are the shelf supports; glue and screw them to the two plywood pieces. These will become the two ends (see figure P6.3). Attach the bottom one-by-three shelf support ¾ inch from the bottom of the plywood so that the base of the cart will be flush with the bottom of the ends. The center one-by-three is fixed at whatever height you would like the center shelf to be. The top one-by-three is attached far enough down from the top so that the one-by-six edging, when lined up with the end at the top (see figure P6.1), will just cover the bottom edge of the shelf support. It's best to make these measurements using the actual pieces of wood. Lumber bought at a yard as one-by-three or one-by-six will measure

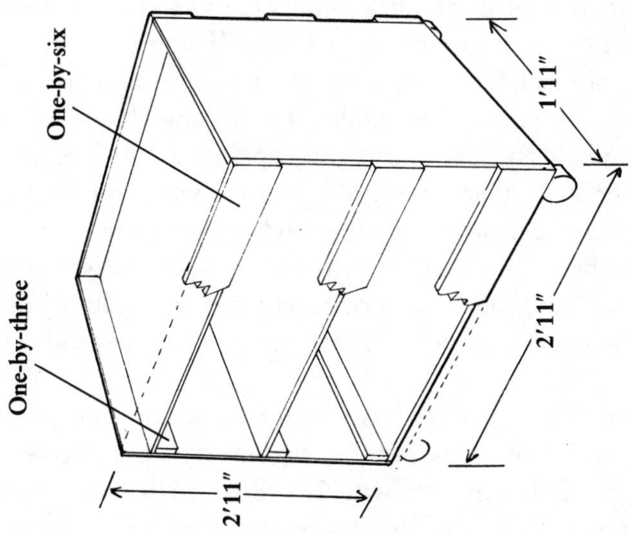

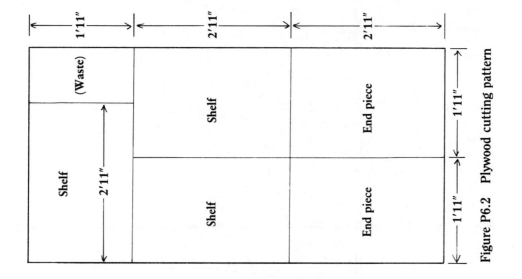

Figure P6.2 Plywood cutting pattern

Figure P6.1 Dimensions

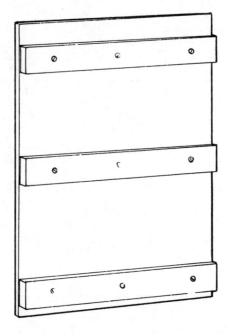

Figure P6.3   End pieces

somewhat less than the full 3 or 6 inches. Make both ends identical in all dimensions; this will ensure the assembled cart is square and upright.

Next, the three shelves are attached to the two ends by being glued and screwed down to the upper edges of the shelf supports. Screw the bottom shelf to the bottom edge of its support. It will be a great help if you can clamp the assembly together while you do this (use a pair of bar or pipe clamps to hold the two ends tightly against the shelves). If you have no clamps long enough, place one end against a wall and keep the assembly together by pressing against the other end as you work.

It is the one-by-six shelf edging that will give the cart strength and ensure its squareness. Therefore they must be cut very carefully so that their ends (flush with the outside of the cart) are perfectly square and are exactly the right length.

When the six edging pieces have been cut, lay the cart on its side, and, having first pre-drilled screw holes in the one-by-sixes, screw them both to the ends of the shelf supports with No. 8 wood screws. Then drill screw holes and screw the edges of the shelves and the end pieces together. Two-inch-long No. 8 wood screws should be used, one every 9 inches or so along the shelf. If the screw holes have been sufficiently countersunk, it should be possible to drive the screws in so that the heads are flush with the surface of the wood.

Now turn the cart upside down and mount small casters at each corner. They will come with a base plate to be screwed to the bottom shelf.

After sanding all the rough edges, you can paint or stain the entire cart. You may want to attach a pair of metal handles near the tops of the ends.

PROJECT 7

A Sleeping Loft

This project is by its nature more permanent than freestanding furniture and is decidedly more structural. As a result, permission to build it may be required from landlords or local building authorities. Ideally, there should be at least 6 feet below the finished loft and 4½ feet above it. More height would be better, and may be required by local codes, but even if permission is not necessary, the loft will not provide any really practical space unless you have these minimum heights to work with.

There are two basic forms a sleeping loft can take: built across the end of a room, or supported on at least one side or corner by a post. How wide a space can be spanned by the front of a sleeping loft depends on the practicality of installing the appropriate supports. For normal residential construction, more than 12 feet will usually require the support of a post. The safest course is to prepare a design and check it with the local building department. What follows is an explanation of the principles involved; the exact dimensions of the various structural members and their relative spacing should conform to local codes.

In essence, a sleeping loft is simply another floor. But unlike most other floors in the house it is not supported on all four sides by walls. Where it does meet a wall, it will rest on a substantial ledger strip securely bolted to the wall. In a wood-frame house a ledger strip is easily attached with long screws called lag bolts to the vertical framing members (called studs), which are commonly spaced 16 inches apart. The only tricks are to make sure that the ledger is well bolted to the studs and is perfectly level. In houses with masonry walls, the bolts must be screwed into lead anchors or plugs set in holes drilled into the masonry.

The loft's frame can then rest on top of the ledger or be attached directly to it with joist hangers (see figure P7.1). The frame itself is simply a series of joists, usually placed 16 inches apart, made of two-by-sixes, two-by-eights, or heavier timbers, depending on the distance to be spanned. The floor itself, made of plywood, is then laid on the joists.

A small sleeping loft may be framed out simply by supporting the joists on the ledger, but if they are longer than 8 feet, you'll have to put blocking between the joists to keep them from twisting or warping.

If, as is usually most practical, the joists run from side wall to side wall across the loft space, a double joist will be at the front of the framing system. This is known as the header; it needs to be stronger than the other joists. Indeed, if the space being spanned is too wide, a separate beam, known as a girder, may be called for. If so, the whole joist system will rest on it.

It is often easier to use a post to support an extra-wide span rather than getting involved with a separate girder. If the loft is being built against less

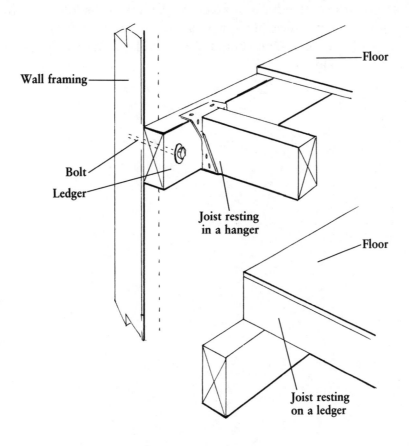

Figure P7.1 Loft framing

than three walls, a post will be essential. A loft designed for a single sleeping space will not pose much of a load-bearing problem, but in building larger lofts, you must position the post carefully. The post is only as strong as its support point. It should be positioned directly over a substantial structural member such as a joist or a girder. If none exists where the post is to be placed, then provision must be made in the form of extra joists or posts in the floor below. This may be no problem if the loft is being built on the ground floor and there is easy access to the basement or foundation below. If there is another room below the loft's location, however, a post may be inappropriate.

The floor of the sleeping loft may simply be ¾-inch plywood nailed directly to the framing joists, but you can also use solid wood flooring. If you choose plywood, be sure that any separate sheets meet over a joist, not between two joists. The ceiling below the loft can be finished with gypsum wallboard, especially if the space is large and you want it to seem a separate room. You may even want to have wiring put in for outlets or fixtures; have this work done by a qualified electrician.

What remains is some form of access to the loft. If the loft is not high, a simple ladder might suffice, but a more ambitious loft calls for proper stairs, complete with handrail. You should also consider a rail along any unprotected side of the loft.

PROJECT 8

An Under-Bed Roll-Out

Most beds are fairly close to the floor and permit only a relatively shallow pull-out unit to be stored underneath. Since the square footage under even a single bed is relatively large, however, even a shallow unit can represent a lot of storage. To make best use of the space, what is needed is a large, if shallow, tray or drawer that is easily rolled or slid out.

The heart of the unit is its firm base. Standard ¾-inch plywood is rigid enough, particularly if you divide the space under the bed between two units, each of which rolls out separately.

Out of a four-by-eight sheet of plywood cut, or have cut, two pieces that measure 2 feet by 3 feet. These will make two units that will fit nicely in the space beneath a single bed. For larger beds (such as double, queen, or king-size beds), consider making four units to fill the space, two on each side. This assumes there is sufficient access from both sides. For beds in particularly cramped quarters, you may have to reduce the depth if a full-size unit cannot be pulled out far enough to reach its entire surface.

For the simplest of roll-outs, just attach a small caster to each corner of the plywood. Sanding the edges and perhaps giving the unit a coat of paint may improve its looks, but for storing a couple of extra blankets or a quilt this is all that is necessary.

To store smaller items, however, you'll do better having a unit with sides, and maybe even partitions. To make sides, use so-called one-inch lumber (¾-inch thick) as wide as the space left between the platform and the bottom of the bed. Standard widths of one-inch lumber range from 4 inches to 12 inches wide, increasing by 2-inch increments. Attach the sides by gluing and screwing up through the plywood (see figure P8.1). If the sides are deeper than 4 inches, they should be glued and screwed to the edges, not the top, of the plywood. Connecting them this way will stiffen the plywood and help it resist sagging under a heavy load. However, if you attach the sides to the edges of the plywood, you must reduce the overall dimensions of the plywood base accordingly. For the best appearance, cut the front piece long enough so it will overlap the two side pieces. Attach the four sides to each other at the corners, using countersunk wood screws in predrilled holes (see figure P8.2).

For a more sophisticated unit, you can add partitions to the unit, then make a cover, using a large piece of plywood as you did for the base. Finally, attach knobs or handles to the front.

If the bed is high enough off the floor to allow a deeper box to be kept underneath, then the order of construction should be altered. If the sides are a foot or so high, begin by cutting these from a sheet of plywood. Glue and screw the corners together (see figure P8.3). Then cut a base piece to fit and glue and screw it to the bottom of the sides. The top should be cut so

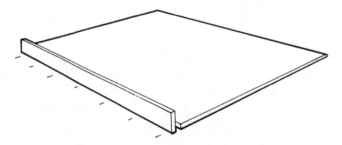

Figure P8.1   Attaching sides no greater than 4 inches high

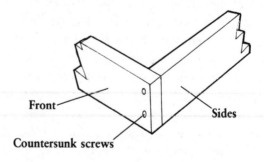

Front

Sides

Countersunk screws

Figure P8.2   Corner detail

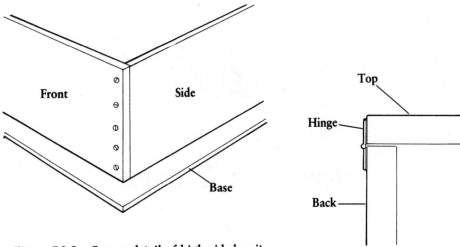

Figure P8.3   Corner detail of high-sided unit

Figure P8.4   Hinging

that it is flush with the box on all sides except the front; an overhang of 1 inch at the front will allow you to lift up the cover easily when the unit is rolled out. Since the unit is designed to spend most of its life under the bed, attaching the top to the back with surface hinges (see figure P8.4) is sufficient.

PROJECT 9

A Small
Over-Door Cabinet

Space tends to be limited in bathrooms, but often you can use what seems like inaccessible space, since the items to be stored, such as medicines and first-aid equipment, are not used frequently. The space above the door is a good place to begin.

Using the entire height between the top of the door frame and the ceiling will usually allow a cabinet from 1 to 2 feet high. Unless the wall is tiled this high, or unless there is an obtrusive molding running around the wall at this height, it won't be hard to attach the cabinet to the wall, especially since the molding at the top of the door can usually be used as a ledge on which to rest the bottom of the cabinet. That should not be the main means of support, however. In wood-framed buildings there are studs at either side of every door opening; these usually extend to the ceiling. In addition, there are substantial "headers" across the top of the door opening. If the cabinet is built just a little wider than the actual door, you'll be able to use these framing members as supports to which the cabinet can be attached securely.

If the doorway is close to a corner, it may be a good idea to extend the cabinet right up to the corner wall so you can attach it there as well. Such additional support will make it possible to increase the depth of the cupboard to as much as 2 feet without complicated supporting joinery. If the doorway is in the middle of a wall and the sides of the cupboard will be unsupported, then it should be no deeper than 18 inches.

To avoid ugly supporting brackets, the body of the cabinet must be constructed so it is sturdy enough to hold heavy items without pulling apart. The simplest way to do this is to join the corners so that the bottom rests *in* the sides, using the simple joint shown in Figure P9.1.

This joint can be made easily in either ¾-inch-thick solid wood, plywood, or composition board. It will be far easier to make if you have access to a table saw or at least a portable circular saw. First, cut the sides to the length desired. Then, from the same width material, cut the top and bottom pieces to a length of the outside dimension of the cabinet *less 1 inch.* This inch represents the half inch that will be added by both of the sides.

The ends of the top and bottom pieces must now be carefully measured, marked, and cut to the dimensions shown in Figure P9.2. Take care that the tongues left at the ends of the boards are ¼-inch thick and ¼-inch deep; this will ensure that there is a full half inch left in the matching upright. It is important to cut these tongues first, before cutting the matching grooves in the uprights; if the tongues are not absolutely perfect, it is easier to adjust the grooves, making them either a little wider or a little narrower as needed. Figure P9.2 also shows how the sides should be cut. Note that the groove should be cut so the tongue fits it snugly but not so tightly that it has to be forced in. If the wood below the groove is broken off, the whole purpose of the joint is destroyed.

When all four corners have been made, cover the grooves and the tongues lightly with glue. Too much glue will simply make assembly difficult and result in a messy cleanup of extruded glue. Then clamp the box together

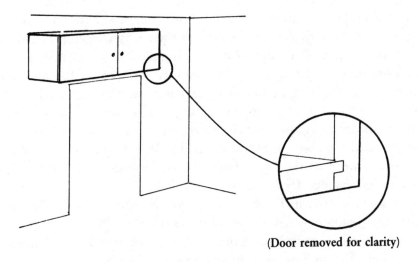

(Door removed for clarity)

Figure P9.1   Corner joint

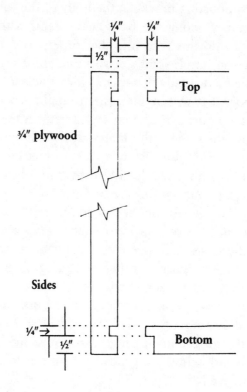

Figure P9.2   Dimensions of joint

with a pair of pipe clamps or bar clamps, making sure the top and bottom are seated properly in their grooves at both front and back. As you tighten the clamps make sure to keep the cabinet square by checking with a square from time to time. When the joints are all pulled up snugly, drive 1½-inch long finishing nails through the sides into the ends of the top and bottom. Nail every 6 inches or so, and, taking care that the nails are lined up so they enter the center of the tongued piece, angle each pair of nails toward each other, as shown in Figure P9.3. If the cabinet is made of solid wood rather than plywood it's best to predrill the nail holes, using a bit slightly smaller than the diameter of the nails. That will avoid splitting the board. Let the glued, nailed cabinet dry for at least 24 hours.

A back made of ½-inch plywood, cut to size, can now be nailed on. If it is absolutely square, it will ensure that the cabinet will be square.

Doors are most easily made from two panels of plywood and attached in the manner of many kitchen cabinet doors with surface-mounted hinges. If the cabinet does, in fact, extend to the ceiling, you'll have to make the doors

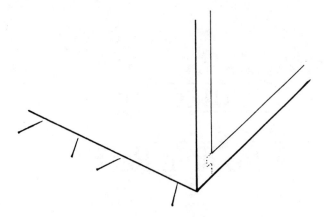

Figure P9.3   Nailing

a little shorter at the top so that they will not scrape the ceiling when opened and closed. When the whole cupboard has been assembled and sanded, it should be given a prime coat and one or two finish coats of oil-base, semigloss paint, since the bathroom can be a steamy place. Install handles and door catches last.

PROJECT 10

A Reading Rack

A reading rack is a simple and adaptable project that can be designed to fit almost any size of wall space. The example shown (see figure P10.1) can easily be enlarged; it can be lengthened, made deeper, or even be made taller if you'd like it to hold large reading materials, such as oversize magazines.

Start with the sides. If you plan to paint the finished piece, use ¾-inch-thick plywood. If you plan a natural finish, choose two pieces (or one piece that can be cut in two) of wood with your favorite tone and graining. Material ¾-inch thick is ideal, but thicker pieces will also work.

The base should be made of the same material, and be as deep from front to back as the side pieces, which are 6 inches in our example. The length of the base can be whatever will fit the space available, up to 2 feet; any longer and it might begin to sag under heavy loads.

You can simply butt the base against the side pieces and screw or nail them together, but a better-looking and stronger job will result if the ends of the base are fitted into grooves (dadoes) cut in the ends (see figure P10.2).

The groove should be as wide as the base is thick. The base should fit the groove snugly, neither too loose nor too tight. You should be able to press the base into the groove by hand, but the fit should be good enough so that if held upside down the base will not fall out. Too loose and the piece will have no strength; too tight and you run the risk of breaking the joint when forcing it together. The base need not be perfectly horizontal from front to back; by tilting the groove, you can position the base at almost any angle. A tilt to the front may help display the contents of the rack. If you decide

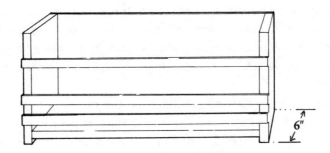

Figure P10.1   Reading rack

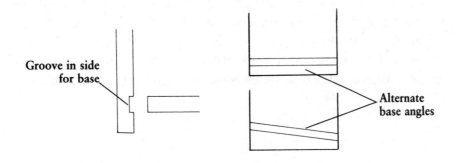

Figure P10.2   Base joint

on a sloping base, however, note that it will need to be deeper than the sides.

Two further caveats: the groove that houses the ends of the base should be at least an inch from the bottom of the sides. And it should be no deeper than a third of the wood's thickness in which it is made. If these two precautions are kept in mind, the construction should be strong, especially when glued and secured with two or three small finishing nails on each side. These nails should be set just below the surface with a nail set, and the resulting cavity filled with wood filler that matches the color of your wood as closely as possible.

The back can be made of ¼-inch plywood. If special wood has been used for the base and sides, don't use common ¼-inch ply. Ask at the lumberyard for ¼-inch mahogany plywood. This material is commonly used as backing for better grades of furniture. It has a better color and grain and will give a more finished look to the rack. In any event, the back should be carefully cut to size and glued to the back of the base and sides before being nailed with many small brads. This is important, since the rack will be attached to the wall through the back, which must therefore be firmly attached.

If you plan to keep only books in your reading rack, then there may be no need for any bars across the front. Books will not fall out, and the back, being secured to the wall, will give the piece sufficient rigidity. But if you want to use the rack for magazines, something must be fixed across the front of the rack. Clear acrylic screwed to the front edges of the sides through predrilled holes with chromed, round-head screws will give the rack a contemporary look as well as making it possible to see the fronts of any items in the rack.

Strips of one-inch slatting, available in the molding bin of most lumberyards, will work equally well. If you use slats, it is even more important to predrill the holes in the end, whether you use screws or nails to attach these pieces. There is always the danger of splitting wood when nailing it near the end. And if you have used hardwood, such as oak, for the sides, it may be difficult to nail or screw into such dense material without predrilling holes.

When finished, the rack can either be painted or, if you have used attractive wood, given two or three coats of varnish to protect it from the dampness and moisture common in bathrooms. Screws inserted through the back will be sufficient to attach the rack to the wall, provided they coincide with studs or are screwed into wall plugs.

PROJECT 11

A Grocery Bag Rack

It is both economically and ecologically sound to recycle as much of our "waste" products as possible, even the humble grocery bag. By making this convenient rack for the bags, you can at least ensure the maximum use for a product that would otherwise be wasted.

Most grocery store paper bags are no larger than 12 inches wide by 17 inches high. A rack to hold the bags will fit behind most base-cabinet doors. The cabinet below the kitchen sink is often convenient for such a rack since the storage space here is usually limited by the sink's plumbing. A rack for bags can be the best way to use this awkward space.

Start by making two sides of ¾-inch plywood. Each side should be 10 inches high, 4 inches wide at the bottom, and 6 inches wide at the top (see figure P11.1). It's best to measure and cut one side, then use it as a pattern for the other. Then you'll be sure the sides match. Note that the distances are measured off at a right angle from the perpendicular back (use a square).

The base, which is also made of ¾-inch-thick plywood, should be 4 inches deep, to match the sides (at the bottom). How wide, from one side to the other, you make the base depends on the width of the door to which you are going to attach the rack. Thirteen inches is wide enough to hold most bags easily, but if the door is much wider you can make a wider rack, to hold more bags.

Nail the bottom of the sides to the ends of the base with 1½-inch-long box nails (thin nails with flat heads, which are well suited for plywood).

Quarter-inch-thick plywood will do perfectly well for the back. But don't

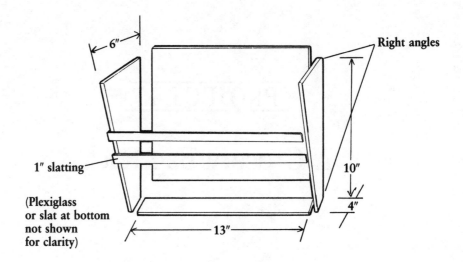

Figure P11.1 Dimensions of grocery bag rack

buy a whole sheet, use whatever is closest to hand. Most lumberyards keep scraps and cut sheets of various sizes and thicknesses. Cut the back to overlap the sides and base, then nail it on.

Across the front of the rack, attach either a low, solid front piece, or (as shown in figure P11.1) several 1-inch-wide slats. Make sure the bottom slat is not too far from the base, for stored bags can easily curl up and slide out under the bottom slat.

In attaching the rack to the cabinet door, be careful not to use screws that are too long. Cabinet doors are frequently less than ½ inch thick. Use a spirit level to establish a horizontal line on the door to position the rack, or measure from the bottom up equally to two spots and connect them to create the line.

PROJECT 12

A Saucepan Pull-Out Unit

The saucepan pull-out unit is designed and made as a freestanding cabinet to fit the awkward space between the side of the range and the adjacent wall. Minimum space for the cabinet is about 12 inches, wide enough to hold a medium-size pot. The actual width, however, should be custom-made to fit the available space.

Start by making the base, as shown in Figure P12.1. The front piece should be as wide as the available space; the depth should reach from the wall to a point 3 inches short of the front of the stove.

Toe space (created by the base) is usually as high as a two-by-four on edge. Using two-by-fours nailed together, as shown, will make an excellent base for the unit.

On the base is a simple cabinet, made of ¾-inch plywood pieces nailed together. The cabinet should be as deep as the stove, less an inch for the front of the cabinet. The sides should be glued and nailed to the top and bottom pieces so that, when assembled, the overall width of the cabinet is the same as the base, to which it is then nailed from the inside. The overall height, from the floor to the top of the cabinet, should be ¾ inch *less* than the height of the stove, so the top, which will be attached later, will be at the same height as the stove top.

The next step is to make the pull-out unit itself. This is very much like making a bookcase (see project 1), but the pull-out is made of plywood. Allow clearance all around. The two end pieces (see figure P12.2) should be 1¾ inches *narrower* than the inside width of the cabinet. This measurement

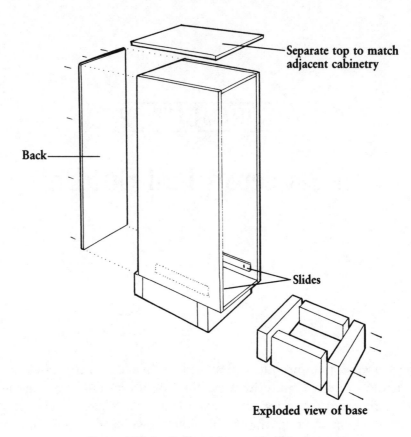

Figure P12.1   Pull-out base and cabinet

is critical, since you have to allow for the ¾-inch-thick back as well as providing a half inch on either side for the drawer slides, which attach the unit to the cabinet. When calculating the height of the pull-out unit, allow for a ¼-inch clearance at both top and bottom (½ inch total), so that there will be no danger of the unit binding in the cabinet. Note also that the unit should be ½ inch shallower than the inside depth of the cabinet.

The slides are attached to the bottom of the back of the pull-out, and to a 4-inch base piece fitted under the bottom shelf (see figure P12.2). Allowing for this base piece, arrange for shelves at convenient heights for the saucepans and pots that will be stored here.

Having put the pull-out unit together and attached the back to it, you must install the slides. There are several varieties available in hardware stores, but they all attach similarly. Follow templates and guides provided with them to ensure their correct alignment. The important thing is to use slides that will extend far enough so the pull-out unit is fully revealed and that are rated for slightly more weight than you judge the unit will ever have to carry.

Now make the front of the unit. It is attached to the front end by being

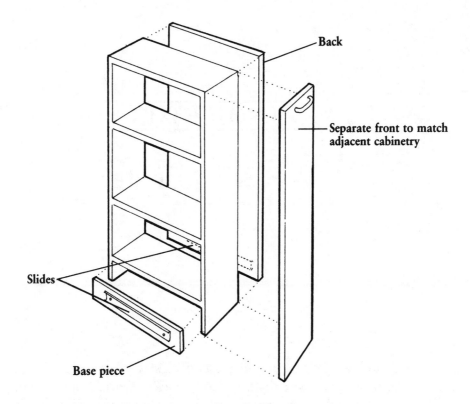

Figure P12.2   Pull-out unit

screwed to it from the inside. It will probably look best if you can match the fronts of the rest of the cabinetry in the kitchen. If these are very complicated, it may be possible to have a matching front custom-made at a cabinet shop or obtain one from the original cabinet supplier.

The reason for making the pull-out unit shallower than the cabinet should now become clear. When the front, which should be as wide as the outside dimension of the cabinet, is attached, it will form a stop for the unit so that the front will close neatly against the front edge of the cabinet.

A similar procedure may now be followed for the top. Ideally this should match the other counter surfaces in the kitchen. A good alternative is to cover a ½-inch-thick piece of plywood with heat-resistant ceramic tile. This provides an additional resting place on which hot pots and pans may be set down. The top, however it is made, should be the same width as the cabinet and extend over the top edge of the front to create an overhang that matches the other counters. Attach it by screwing into it from within the cabinet.

PROJECT 13

A Sewing Center

A rollabout sewing center provides not only a place to store a sewing machine and associated paraphernalia but also a place to work. If it's easy to get to work, you're more likely to embark on a project than if setting up and putting away is a long process. The sewing center will house a sewing machine, provide a work surface, and create a place to keep all the bits and pieces that are part of sewing. At the same time it remains a neat, self-contained, easily moved unit.

The dimensions given (see figure P13.1) are typical for average situations. You may need to adjust them to suit your particular machine or the particular countertop under which the unit is to be stored.

The cabinet is constructed either of good ¾-inch plywood or medium-density particleboard. Particularly with particleboard, the screw holes should be predrilled to avoid any danger of splitting. Start with the two side pieces. The suggested 28 inches is a good work height that will also allow the unit to fit under most countertops. In certain circumstances you may have to reduce this height. Similarly, you may have to alter the depth of 18 inches, as conditions dictate.

Cut the two horizontal pieces (the shelf and the bottom) 24½ inches long, and glue and screw them to the sides. Set the bottom flush with the bottom edge of the sides, and position the shelf so that enough room is left above it to house your sewing machine under a slide-out top. The top will need 2¾ inches clearance, so add this to the height of the sewing machine when calculating how far down from the top the shelf should be.

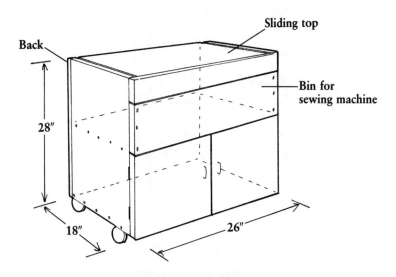

Figure P13.1   Sewing center dimensions

It is the back piece that will give the unit its strength and stability, so make sure this piece is cut accurately and glued and screwed to the back edges of the sides, the bottom, and the shelf, with all edges flush. No. 8 1½-inch wood screws are fine for assembling these pieces. If you countersink the pilot holes a little, the heads can be covered with wood filler prior to painting, which will give the unit a neat, finished appearance.

Across the front of the unit, starting 2¾ inches down from the top (to allow for the slide-out top), and with its bottom edge flush with the bottom of the central shelf, glue and screw the front fixed panel in the same way as the back was attached.

You will now have created a bin for the sewing machine at the top, and storage space at the bottom that can be left open, fitted with removable wire trays or bins, or closed off with a pair of flush doors as shown (see figure P13.1). If you elect to fit doors, they should be cut so that they are flush with the outside of the unit and the lower edge of the bottom. Various hinges can be used: surface-mounted kitchen cabinet hinges are perhaps the easiest to install, but ¾-inch cabinet hinges may give a better appearance. To use the latter, you'll have to cut shallow mortises (see figure P13.2). Since the bottoms of the doors close against the bottom of the unit, you can use easy-to-install magnetic door catches. They are simply surface mounted (see figure P13.3), leaving the front of the doors with a clean appearance, except for the necessary handles.

The slide-out top, upon which the sewing machine will rest when in use, is made next (see figure P13.4). Start with the top itself, which should be as

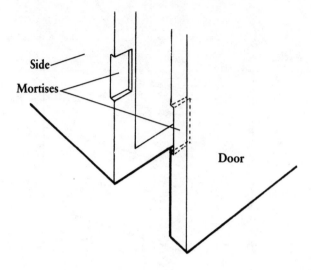

Figure P13.2 Hinge mortises

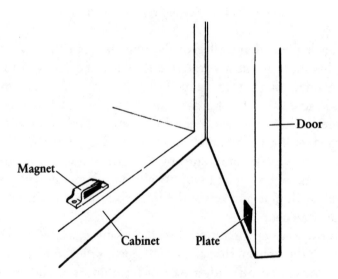

Figure P13.3 Magnetic catch

deep as the sides. (The front piece, to be added later, will make the top flush at the front with the rest of the unit.) Its width will equal the distance between the sides, less a ⅛-inch clearance on either side. Under each side, ½ inch in from each end, attach a piece that measures exactly 2 inches deep. Then across the front attach another piece; it should be measured to cover the front edges of the top and the two side pieces just attached. This front piece should be as wide as the overall width of the unit. All this can be followed in Figure P13.4. Drawer slides rated to carry the weight of your particular sewing machine are now installed at the outside of the side pieces and the inside of the unit itself. Locate the slides carefully so that the top is flush with the top of the cabinet's sides.

All that remains, apart from a light sanding of all edges and painting, is to attach casters to the bottom of the unit, at each corner. Since you don't want the unit to move away from you when in use, it is best to use self-locking casters, so the unit will be immobile once it has been rolled into place.

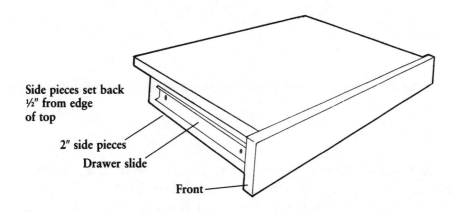

**Side pieces set back
½″ from edge
of top**

2″ side pieces

Drawer slide

Front

Figure P13.4   Slide-out top

PROJECT 14

An Over-Stairwell
Storage Unit

This project involves fairly simple carpentry with a little finish work. Most stairwells are rectangular, and the space above the landing is usually three-sided (see figure P14.1). Given this situation, there is room for the storage unit proposed. Obviously, not all stairwells will have the same dimensions, but the construction program described here will be applicable to many.

The most important point to bear in mind in planning such a unit is to leave sufficient headroom under the unit. The minimum safe headroom is 6½ feet, although local building codes should be checked for regional differences.

Given a rectangular space, bounded on three sides by walls, the first step is to attach to each side a ledger strip on which the floor of the cupboard will rest, and to which the ceiling under the cupboard will be affixed. If you are working in a wood-frame house, first locate the studs, the vertical framing members to which the interior wall covering is nailed. If the walls are paneled with wood, you can often tell where the studs are by visible nailheads or seams between sections of paneling. But if the walls are covered with gypsum wallboard that has been well finished, there will be no such clues. In that case, use a hand-held stud detector, which magnetically finds nails in the studs, or make an educated guess and test it by trying a nail in the area inside the future storage unit. Base your guess on the fact that the studs are normally spaced 16 inches apart and that there must always be studs in

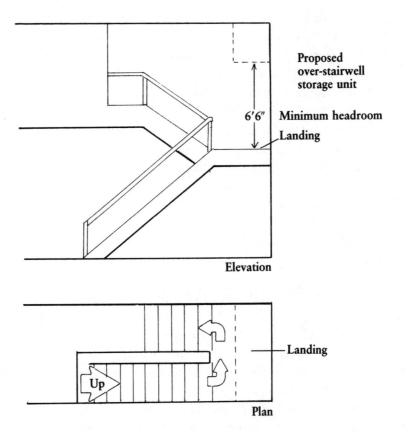

Figure P14.1   Typical stairwell landing

every corner, at either side of door or window openings, and very frequently next to electrical outlets.

A two-by-four will form a sufficient ledger if nailed to every stud with 12-penny nails. Bearing the height restriction in mind, use a spirit level to mark a perfectly horizontal line around the top of the stairwell where the ledger is to be located. With help from another person, if necessary, hold the two-by-four to the line, and nail at one end first. Then, using the level to double-check the ledger's position against the line (it is surprising how these things can vary), nail the rest of it securely to the wall. A word of caution regarding electrical wiring: if there are any outlets in the area, or if you have any other reason to suspect that there may be wiring running through the wall where you intend to nail, turn off the power before nailing. If you happen to hit a wire, the circuit breaker will trip when you turn the power back on.

Attach a ledger on each of the three sides, then nail a header, consisting of two two-by-fours nailed together, across the fourth, open side (see figure

P14.2). If you happen to have an area where all four sides are enclosed, then simply attach a ledger around the entire circumference. The floor of the cupboard is supported on more two-by-fours spaced 16 inches apart "on center" (the distance from the *center* of one two-by-four to the *center* of the next should measure exactly 16 inches). Any odd spacing should be less than 16 inches, not more. Note that the outside two-by-four should measure 16 inches from its *outside* edge (not its center) to the center of the next one. Placing the two-by-four like this not only ensures sufficient support but also makes it much easier to use covering materials such as gypsum wallboard and plywood, which are commonly manufactured in sheets that measure exact multiples of 16 inches.

It doesn't make much difference which way you set these two-by-fours—front to back or side to side. Choose the direction that ensures the most economical use of the material; two-by-fours are sold in many lengths.

The ends of the two-by-fours can be toenailed (see figure P14.3) to the ledger or they can be attached with hangers that are nailed first to the ledger, then to the ends of the two-by-fours. Toenailing is immeasurably easier if you have predrilled the piece *before* hammering it into place between the ledgers. Once the two-by-fours are in place, it will be simple to nail down a floor of ¾-inch plywood.

The opening at the front of the unit must now be framed out so that it can be fitted with doors. Nail two-by-four uprights (studs) at either side of the opening and across the top. Attach two more two-by-fours, one at either side of the planned door opening. If the space left at either side of the door opening is greater than 16 inches, install additional two-by-fours every 16 inches as required. The new ceiling (beneath the unit) and the walls of the front around the door can now be covered with gypsum wallboard (or wall covering similar to that on the walls in the surrounding area).

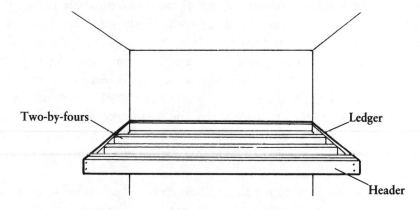

Figure P14.2   Cupboard floor framing

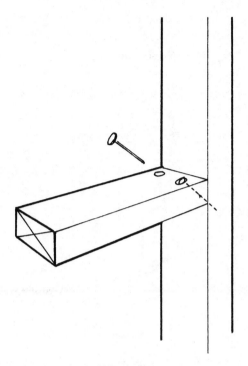

Figure P14.3   Toenailing

The easiest way to make doors is to use panels cut from ¾-inch plywood, hinged to the side of the opening. If you can handle more sophisticated joinery, add a one-by-six frame around the inside of the opening. Finish it with one-by-four trim on the outside, to cover the gap between the frame and the wall (see figure P14.4). For a more finished look, install a pair of louvered doors (they come in many sizes).

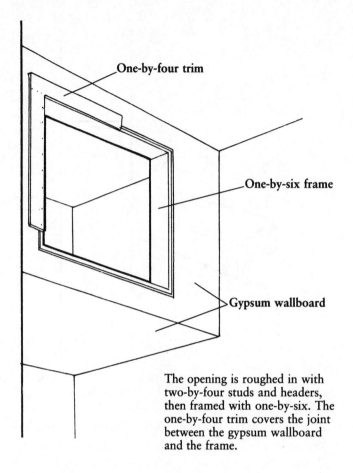

One-by-four trim

One-by-six frame

Gypsum wallboard

The opening is roughed in with two-by-four studs and headers, then framed with one-by-six. The one-by-four trim covers the joint between the gypsum wallboard and the frame.

Figure P14.4   Framing and trimming opening

PROJECT 15

Enlarging
an Attic Trapdoor

This project involves certain carpentry skills and should not be undertaken unless you already own and know how to use the basic carpentry tools. An attic trapdoor is invariably located between two ceiling joists that have had headers installed between them to define a small, rectangular opening (see figure P15.1). This opening is often not large enough for easy access. To enlarge it, you must cut one side of the opening and push one end back as well.

Whenever a framing member—a ceiling joist in this case—has a section removed (as for this trapdoor opening), the piece against which it now ends (called a header) should be doubled. At the same time, the joists on either side of the cut joist should also be doubled. (These are now properly called trimmers.) This doubling of the members that defines the opening provides the strength that was lost through the removal of a section of the framing (see figure P15.2).

A small opening, such as that shown in Figure P15.1, may well not have had such doubling, or at least not on all four sides. But when the opening is enlarged, doubling is required. Before cutting through the joist on this side, however, provide some support underneath, at what will be both ends of the new opening. A two-by-four placed up against the ceiling, supported by a vertical post, will suffice.

Working from the attic, cut out a section of joist sufficient to create the opening size required, remembering that part of it will be used up by doubled headers. If you can manage to leave the ceiling intact at this stage, it will be

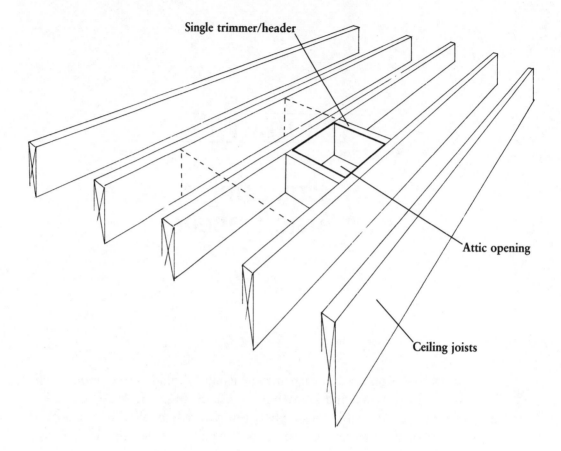

Figure P15.1   Attic opening

easier to trim it to size when the headers have been installed. Make headers from the same size lumber as the existing joists. Nail the doubled lengths together before fitting them in place, and nail into their ends through the sides of the joists between which they fit.

Now it is time to double the joists at either side of the new opening. Ideally, an extra piece should be attached to the entire joist, from one end to the other. However, doing this may be difficult or impossible because it means removing numerous crosspieces that might butt up against the original joist. Double as much of the joist as you can.

When the new opening has been thus framed out, carefully saw through the ceiling so that it now finishes flush with the inside of the doubled headers and trimmers. Make sure that the ceiling is nailed around the new opening, and, if necessary, add trim to replace any that existed around the old opening. This may involve making a new frame around the inside of the opening, to which trim, covering the edge of the cut ceiling, is attached, and to which a ledger, supporting the trapdoor, is nailed.

A new trapdoor is, of course, also needed. The easiest way to build a trapdoor is to make a frame of two-by-fours and cover one side with gypsum wallboard. The edges should be protected with metal corner guard. The trapdoor can then simply rest on the ledger fixed inside the frame, or be hinged at one side if the opening is large enough to permit—and has been fitted with—a fold-down ladder or staircase.

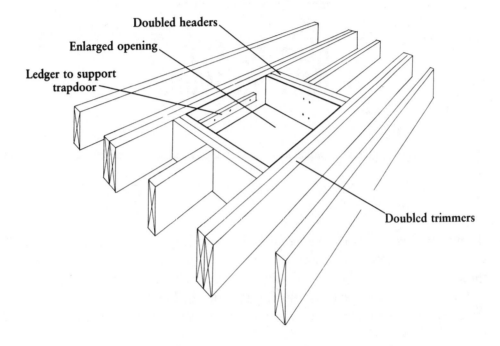

Figure P15.2   Framing for enlarged attic trapdoor

PROJECT 16

Furring Out
Basement Walls

If your basement walls are made of poured concrete or concrete block, furring them out and adding insulation will create a better storage environment. At the same time, it will allow you to finish the walls, improving the appearance of the basement and actually making it easier to build shelving and other storage units. (It is far easier to nail such things to wood studs than to concrete blocks.)

"Furring out" simply means building a wood framework attached to the face of the masonry walls. It is done in such a way that insulation can be installed within this framework and finished wall material attached to it.

There are two basic methods, depending on what type of insulation you intend to use. The first uses a framework of one-by-threes or two-by-twos, within which are fixed sheets of rigid polystyrene insulation (a lightweight foam board). This is perhaps the quicker and slightly easier method. The second method, which uses two-by-fours to create the framework, allows the use of thicker, fiberglass insulation, in batt or roll form. Moreover, it provides a stronger base to which any subsequent built-ins can be attached more easily.

If you elect to install rigid insulation, the furring-strip framework must be at least the same thickness as the insulation, either 1 or 2 inches. It is easiest to construct a regular pattern of uprights and horizontals based on the sheet size of the insulation, starting from one end of the largest uninterrupted wall (see figure P16.1). The insulation boards are easily cut to fit around windows and other openings and obstructions.

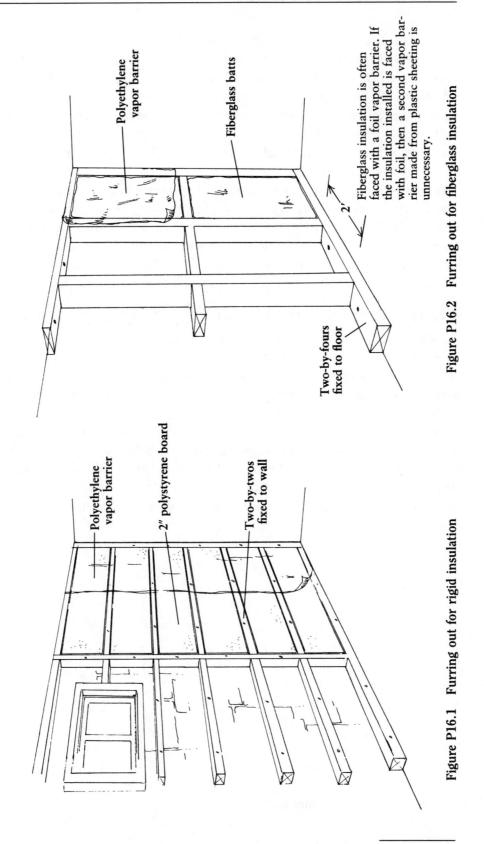

Polyethylene
vapor barrier

Fiberglass batts

Fiberglass insulation is often
faced with a foil vapor barrier. If
the insulation installed is faced
with foil, then a second vapor barrier made from plastic sheeting is
unnecessary.

2'

Two-by-fours
fixed to floor

Figure P16.2   Furring out for fiberglass insulation

Polyethylene
vapor barrier

2" polystyrene board

Two-by-twos
fixed to wall

Figure P16.1   Furring out for rigid insulation

It's possible to attach the furring strips with special masonry nails, hammered in by hand, but if you have an entire basement to furr out it will be easier and much quicker to rent a stud gun. This tool fires special nails with sufficient force to attach even two-by-fours to concrete with ease. Make certain you learn how to operate the gun safely; a clerk in the shop you rent from should be able to instruct you. If you erect the framework carefully enough, the insulation board will be held in place by friction alone until you install the wall covering.

A framework of two-by-fours entails a little more work (see figure P16.2). This is very similar to building a regular freestanding partition wall, except that it is built against an existing concrete wall. It is held in place at the floor and at the ceiling. At the floor, it's nailed through its bottom member, known as the sole plate, into the concrete floor. At the top, the top plate is nailed to the joists of the floor above. Fiberglass insulation, which is made to be installed in two-by-four walls, is made in two widths: 16 and 24 inches. Since you are unlikely to be concerned with strength, 24-inch spacing for the uprights (the studs) will provide an adequate nailing base for typical wall coverings, which can be sheets of gypsum wallboard, plywood paneling, or even solid-wood paneling. An additional advantage of building a two-by-four wall is it has sufficient depth in which to install wiring and electrical outlets, if desired.

Once the framework is erected and the insulation installed, put a vapor barrier over the entire surface before adding the finished wall material. This is a complete layer of polyethylene stapled to the front edge of the studs. Any seams must be taped. This applies to either framework system if the insulation you've installed does not have its own vapor barrier.

PROJECT 17

Garage Shelving

Shelving units in garages need only be sturdy and commodious; there is little point in fine joinery and woodworking techniques. Turning an entire wall into shelf space is ideal and often can be the easiest form of construction, since you can gain support at both ends. But even if only part of a wall is available, some shelves are better than none, and such a unit is still a relatively easy project to undertake.

Items that are stored in garages tend to be bulky and heavy, so make everything out of two-by-twelve construction-grade lumber. This is strong enough to span up to four feet without sagging, even when it supports fairly heavy items. Two-by-twelve is not as expensive, per board foot, as one-inch-thick finished boards.

Since a shelf unit made of two-by-twelve lumber is quite heavy, construct the units in 4-foot-wide modules. This will make each module manageable as you build it and whenever you have to move it around. It also allows you to rearrange or eliminate modules later.

Start by planning the size of the units to fill the space you have. Fit as many 4-foot units into the space as you can. If the remaining space is greater than 2 feet make a separate smaller unit to fit that space. If the remaining space is *less* than 2 feet, lengthen each unit slightly to take up the space.

The uprights should be made first. They should reach from the floor to the ceiling, if it is finished. If it's not, and there are exposed ceiling joists, collar beams, or roof trusses, make the uprights only as high as the top of the wall. At this point there are very often exposed structural members, such as top plates, to which the wall unit can be secured easily.

Unless you know you'll have to store taller items here, making shelves with 12 inches between them is a good average measurement. Any extra space left after dividing the uprights into shelves spaced this way should be added to the bottom shelf—there will always be some items larger than others.

After deciding how many shelves you need, cut them from the same two-by-twelve lumber 45 inches long (46 inches, if you use the dado method of support). With two uprights 1½ inches thick (the finished measure of two-inch lumber) that will give you a module precisely 4 feet in width.

There are three ways to support the shelves (see figure P17.1). The first method (A) is the best, although it entails a little more work and requires the longer shelf measurement. It involves making ½-inch-deep dadoes in the uprights, into which the ends of the shelves will fit. An electric router will make dadoes very quickly and can be set up with a guide so that complete accuracy is ensured. But even without a router, all that is necessary is a handsaw and a chisel. In both cases the important thing is to mark the dadoes carefully before cutting. Remember that you want to leave 12 inches

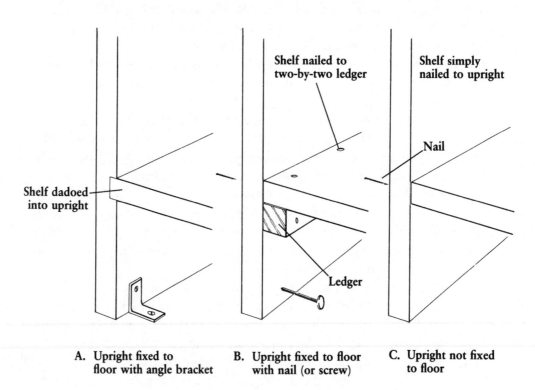

Figure P17.1   Three methods of attaching shelves

between the shelves, so if the two-by-twelve lumber measures 1½ inches thick, you'll need to add this amount to the distance between successive dadoes. To ensure your dadoes match in the uprights, cut and dado each pair of uprights at the same time. Or make a marked rod, the same height as the uprights, that shows the exact location of the dadoes from bottom to top; use this rod and only this rod to mark all the uprights.

The second method (B) still involves marking the exact location of the shelves on the uprights, but instead of making dadoes, two-by-two ledger strips the width of the uprights are nailed to the uprights just at the level of the shelves. The shelves are then nailed to these ledgers. It is a good idea, especially if heavy objects will be stored on these shelves, to also nail through the uprights from the outside into the ends of the shelves.

This, in fact, is the last method (C): simply nail through the uprights into the ends of the shelves. If 12-penny common nails are used to fasten two-inch lumber, the unit will be surprisingly strong and more than adequate for most purposes. But for maximum weight-carrying capacity, choose method A or B.

When all units have been constructed, position the first one against the wall and secure it top and bottom by direct nailing into adjacent exposed framing members or by bolting it to the floor with angle brackets, as shown in Figure P17.1. The second and subsequent units should also be screwed or bolted to the previous unit, as shown. Do not use nails unless you are positive you will never want to move the units. It is necessary to fix adjacent units to one another at only one or two places. The last unit is slid into place and secured to its neighbor and the end wall in the same way as the first unit.

PROJECT 18

A Garage Lean-to

There are several ways to build a lean-to on the side of a garage. The structure can be no more than a simple roof supported by one wall of the garage and two posts, or it can be a substantial addition on its own foundation, with access to it cut into the garage wall. Before starting on anything, check with your building department to make sure that such as extension is permissible. There may be zoning restrictions, such as limits on setbacks from property lines and on the percentage of the property that can be built on, as well as building code regulations that must be observed.

Even for the simplest lean-to, there are two basic considerations: how it is attached on one side, and how it is supported on the other. It is not enough simply to rest a roof against a wall of the garage; it must be firmly attached and supported and, equally important, attached with a waterproof joint.

To support the roof, you can use a ledger strip. This is a horizontal piece, firmly attached to the garage wall, on which the rafters of the lean-to will rest and to which they are attached. If the garage is of wood-frame construction, make sure that the ledger is nailed or bolted to the upright framing members (studs) and not just to the siding.

To ensure a watertight seam between the lean-to roof and the garage wall, the lean-to roof must be properly flashed (see figure P18.1). If you're dealing with a masonry wall this means chipping out the mortar between two courses of concrete block (or brick) immediately above the point where the lean-to's roof abuts the wall. Into this groove you mortar the edge of a metal flashing strip that is then folded down over the top of the new roof. In a wood-frame building, the flashing must be inserted up under adjacent layers of siding, whether this is boards, shingles, clapboards, or other material.

How you support the other three sides of the lean-to depends largely on how cold the winters are and how deep the foundation consequently must be. In areas where any frost is likely, whether mild or severe, the foundation—even if it is just a pier to support a post—must extend deeper into the ground than the maximum frost line. In warm areas of the country a simple block laid on a base of gravel may suffice. In every case, however, there should be some form of masonry, such as a concrete block, small poured footing, or a slab of rock or laid-up stone, between the ground and a wood support of any kind.

A small, 8-foot-square lean-to can be adequately supported by two four-by-four corner posts, which in turn support a doubled two-by-ten header (see figure P18.2). Rafters made of two-by-sixes, spaced 2 feet apart and resting on the ledger at one end and the header at the other end, can support a simple plywood roof, covered with roll roofing.

A more sophisticated lean-to should be constructed on a concrete slab poured to meet the garage foundation. On the slab, simple framed walls of two-by-fours can be built. These are, in turn, covered with some form of

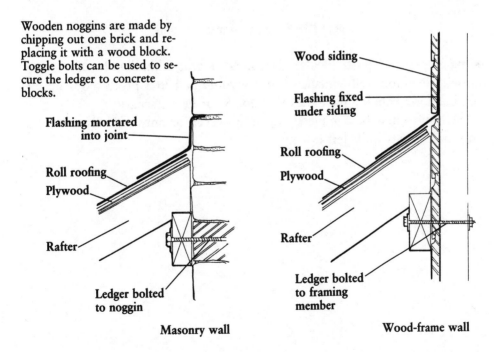

Figure P18.1   Flashing a lean-to roof

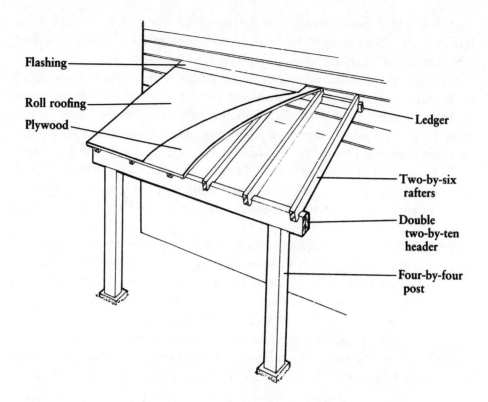

Flashing

Roll roofing

Plywood

Ledger

Two-by-six rafters

Double two-by-ten header

Four-by-four post

Figure P18.2   Small lean-to framing

siding or, perhaps, partially glazed (to create storage that doubles as a green-house). This more fully finished lean-to would be better protected from the weather and probably have lockable doors for better security.

The lean-to may be completely open, however, or only partially enclosed, with one or two walls left open.

PROJECT 19

A Garage Workbench

You can of course buy a workbench that is virtually a piece of furniture, fitted with all manner of vises, shelves, drawers, and racks. Yet even the plainest work surface installed against a garage wall will prove itself valuable in almost any home project.

Building such a simple work surface, or bench, in a garage is usually not difficult because you can attach it to the wall so easily. That's important, because there's a big difference between a table at working height and a workbench. The latter has to be firm and sturdy enough to be worked on, often vigorously. Building the workbench against a wall ensures this.

Start with a two-by-four ledger as long as you intend the workbench to be. Bolt or nail this securely to the wall. Use a spirit level to make sure it is perfectly horizontal. Set the ledger at a height that will bring the finished work surface, after adding the frame and the top, to between 28 and 32 inches high. The exact height will depend on how tall you are. Ideally, you'll be most comfortable if, standing at a bench, you can lay your palm flat on the bench while keeping your arm straight. Thirty inches is considered an acceptable height if various people will be using the bench.

The work surface can be either a plywood top supported on a frame of two-by-fours, or a solid top made from two two-by-twelves laid side by side. The first is easier to build, but the second is somewhat sturdier and may be better if you expect to do a lot of heavy pounding.

To construct a plywood top, prepare a frame consisting of two ends and one side (the ledger strip forms the back side), supported at each corner by a four-by-four to which the two-by-four frame is attached, using lag bolts (see figure P19.1). The bench shown has a frame 2 feet deep. This will prove to be the most economical size, since plywood sheets are commonly 4 feet wide. There is no reason, of course, why the bench shouldn't be a bit deeper. For greatest strength using this kind of construction, include front-to-back two-by-fours at two-foot intervals the entire length of the bench. The bench can extend along an entire wall, provided you add an extra four-by-four support post every 4 feet.

Once the frame is complete, attached to the wall, and given legs, cover the top with plywood cut to be flush with the front and sides of the frame. Half-inch-thick plywood is acceptable, but ¾-inch plywood makes a much better top that will be less likely to give. Nail the plywood down with 1½-inch-long box nails or special plywood nails of a similar length, using a nail every 6 to 8 inches. If more than one sheet is needed to cover the frame, be sure the joint between the sheets falls over a two-by-four.

If you want to make the top out of two two-by-twelves, construct a similar frame, but you'll need the front-to-back supports only every 4 feet (coinciding with the support posts). This bench will be slightly less deep, since a two-by-twelve is only 11½ inches wide. If you make the frame only 20 inches deep, the top will overhang the frame by about 3 inches. This overhang can be very useful to attach bench-edge vises and other items that clamp onto an edge.

For most purposes it will be sufficient to screw or bolt the two-by-twelves

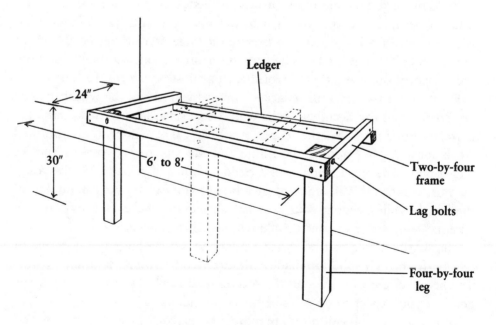

Figure P19.1 Workbench frame

directly to the frame. All wood expands and shrinks somewhat as its moisture content changes, and two boards attached side by side will inevitably develop a crack between them no matter how closely they are fixed to begin with. To prevent that, you could edge-join the boards before you attach them to the frame. Assuming both boards are straight, glue the meeting edges and clamp the boards together until the glue has dried. If they are not straight enough to meet along their entire length, either choose two straighter ones or have the lumberyard "joint" them for you. Many lumberyards offer this service for a nominal fee. It consists of running the edges of the boards across a jointer, which is a machine that produces a perfectly square and straight edge.

Index